Penguin Education
Penguin Science of Behaviour
General Editor: B. M. Foss

Skills, Learning
Editors: Harry Kay and L. J. Postman

Feedback and Human Beh
John Annett

Feedback and Human Behaviour

The effects of knowledge of results, incentives and reinforcement on learning and performance

John Annett

Penguin Books

Penguin Books Ltd, Harmondsworth,
Middlesex, England
Penguin Books Inc., 7110 Ambassador Road,
Baltimore, Md 21207, U.S.A.
Penguin Books Australia Ltd, Ringwood,
Victoria, Australia

First published 1969
Copyright © John Annett, 1969

Made and printed in Great Britain by
Hazell Watson & Viney Ltd,
Aylesbury, Bucks
Set in Linotype Plantin

832240

T   L

Penguin Science of Behaviour

This book is one of the first in an ambitious project, the *Penguin Science of Behaviour*, which will cover a very wide range of psychological inquiry. Many of the short 'unit' texts will be on central teaching topics, while others will deal with present theoretical and empirical work which the Editors consider to be important new contributions to psychology. We have kept in mind both the teaching divisions of psychology and also the needs of psychologists at work. For readers working with children, for example, some of the units in the field of Developmental Psychology will deal with techniques in testing children, other units will deal with work on cognitive growth. For academic psychologists, there will be units in well-established areas such as Learning and Perception, but also units which do not fall neatly under any one heading, or which are thought of as 'applied', but which nevertheless are highly relevant to psychology as a whole.

The project is published in short units for two main reasons. Firstly, a large range of short texts at inexpensive prices gives the teacher a flexibility in planning his course and recommending texts for it. Secondly, the pace at which important new work is published requires the project to be adaptable. Our plan allows a unit to be revised or a fresh unit to be added with maximum speed and minimal cost to the reader.

Above all, for students, the different viewpoints of many authors, sometimes overlapping, sometimes in contradiction, and the range of topics Editors have selected will reveal the complexity and diversity which exist beyond the necessarily conventional headings of an introductory course.

B.M.F.

Contents

Editorial Foreword

Many areas of psychology have been transformed in the last two decades. Old problems that have been in the forefront of human thinking for centuries have been put in a new context and their relationship to other subjects in the biological and technological disciplines has been appreciated. These new ways of conceptualizing such issues has increased our understanding of many psychological subjects and not least those in the field of skills and learning.

Adaptive behaviour was traditionally regarded as the province of biological creatures. The natural world carried this hallmark – its differing species to differing extents displayed the ability to adapt to environmental demands. But not only did they adapt; within the life cycle of the individual member of the species the genetically determined nervous system was capable of improving its adaptive responses with practice. The process then was twofold: adaptation to adaptation. We generally call it learning.

Up to a few years ago man's history recorded no examples of learning outside biological systems. As soon as we turned to physical as opposed to biological matter the process abruptly stopped. Any machine devised by man showed no such learning. But now our whole perspective has suddenly changed. The sharp division between biological and physical systems has been broken. We have become accustomed to the idea that machines will adapt to events, that we can build a system which will retrieve information for us and provide us with the possible solutions to problems. The computer age is under way.

This orientation which has been so much influenced by cybernetics and information theory has permeated our whole approach to human learning. In particular it has changed our way of considering skilled motor responses. We see the human operator carrying out a sequence of responses as analogous to a system which gradually modifies its responses as it gets nearer to its target. The discrepancy between the target and the actual response decides the next response in much the same way as a golfer's error on the putting green decides his next putt.

This book is about one of the oldest puzzles in the study of learning – how information about our actions is able to influence learning. Dr Annett has worked in this field for many years and he has put together a most authoritative account of how psychologists have tackled this problem and how their thinking is now influenced by present communication systems.

H.K.

Preface

When a student is told the result of a test, a golfer sees his ball fall into the rough, or a pieceworker gets his pay packet he is getting knowledge of results. There are few actions which have no perceptible result and in most cases knowledge of results is important to the performer and will affect his future behaviour. The role of knowledge of results in controlling and changing behaviour has been the subject of extensive research for seventy years or more and this book is an attempt to summarize and analyse this work.

Knowledge of results (KR) has a wide variety of manifestations, visual, auditory, and kinaesthetic, sometimes appearing as a numerical score, sometimes as a financial reward, or a nod from the experimenter or a flashing light on a panel. The effects of KR have been investigated in tasks ranging from simple hand movements to the learning of mathematics and even in psychotherapy. In fact KR is one of the most general features of all learning situations. It is also one of the most controversial from a theoretical point of view. To be sure there are few who would deny that KR is a potent factor in efficient learning and in maintaining high levels of performance but the reasons for these effects have long been disputed.

A classical view is that all forms of KR can be regarded as rewarding or punishing and that a rewarding result preserves the behaviour which preceded it by some relatively simple (but as yet unexplained) mechanism. This is reinforcement theory which stresses the motivational aspects of KR and it is firmly based on animal experimentation, where actions such as choosing a particular alley in a maze or pressing a lever a certain number of times are reinforced by tangible rewards such as food.

The analogy between evolutionary theory, the survival of successful species, and learning by selective rewards and punishments makes reinforcement theory attractive, but many difficulties arise when the theory is applied to human learning. It has been suggested that KR gives information rather than, or perhaps in addition to, reinforcement. In recent years many psychologists have been increasingly using terms and concepts derived from cybernetics, of which feedback and information are two of the most important. Knowledge of results is clearly capable of being described as feedback information. The position taken in this book is that the cybernetic analogy is more satisfactory and potentially more fruitful than the evolutionary analogy represented by reinforcement theory.

The introductory chapter is primarily concerned with describing the varieties of KR and setting out some of the theoretical options. The next three chapters review the basic literature in motor, perceptual and verbal tasks. Chapters 5, 6 and 7 attempt to analyse the incentive, reinforcing and informative functions of KR and chapter 8 shows how these can be described in terms of feedback.

It is hoped that the book will be of use to second and third year undergraduates and that postgraduate students and research workers will find it a convenient source of references and perhaps some ideas worth arguing about. Although not primarily intended for the layman the fundamental points at issue, teaching, testing, scoring, giving incentives and rewards, deserve the attention of teachers, industrialists and economists and all those who are concerned with the education and training and (dare one say it) the control of their fellow men.

Acknowledgements

I am particularly grateful to Professor Harry Kay, who suggested I write this book, and to Professor Brian Foss for helpful comments on the draft. I also wish to thank Keith Duncan, Michael Sheldon, Rob Stammers, John Patrick, Mike Gray and Peter Lennie and my wife Marian for their suggestions, and Carol Horton for secretarial help.

1 The Consequences of Behaviour

Behaviour has both antecedents and consequences. Many instances of behaviour seem best described in terms of their antecedents. When we answer the telephone or stop at a red light the telephone bell and the traffic light may be thought of as stimuli which elicited these particular responses. Equally we find instances of behaviour which, in ordinary language at least, seem best described in terms of consequences, instances of behaviour directed towards the achievement of a goal. Thus we lift the receiver and dial a number in order to call someone, put a coin in a vending machine in order to get chocolate, work hard to pass examinations, and so on. The distinction seems to be sensible enough and indeed has been officially recognized in the distinction between *respondent* and *operant* behaviour, but, at the same time, it is undeniable that goal-directed activity is not entirely devoid of antecedent stimuli, and that even behaviour which appears to have been directly elicited by some stimulus does have consequences, and that stimulus, response and result are normally related in a coherent behaviour pattern. Lifting the receiver is not just a response to the telephone bell, the activity stops the noise that it makes and puts one in contact with the caller. In the same way, stimuli such as the feeling of hunger and the sight of the vending machine not only precede but clearly have something to do with putting a coin in the machine.

Although both antecedents and consequences are intimately involved in all coherent behaviour, consequences have generally been assigned a secondary role in the description and analysis of behaviour. Current formulations of behaviour are most often represented in terms of a stimulus leading to a response, s→R. There are several good reasons for this relative stress on antecedent stimulation. The first is that the emergent scientific psychology around the turn of the century found physiologists working with the concept of the reflex, a response which is almost invariably initiated by a specified stimulus. Whilst neurophysiologists have long since abandoned, or at least dramatically modified, the old reflex arc, the concept became deeply embedded in early attempts at a scientific formulation of behaviour. A second and possibly better reason for this emphasis on antecedent stimuli at the expense of consequences, results and goals is the difficulty over teleological explanations. In a deterministic psychology due account has to be taken of the forward direction of causality. Not only is it simpler to offer an antecedent stimulus as the cause of a piece of behaviour, but explanations in terms of events that happen after the behaviour has occurred present logical difficulties which the rigorous psychologist goes to great lengths to avoid. As we shall see modern developments in the theory of servo-mechanisms essentially remove the logical difficulty about integrating consequences and results with antecedent stimuli in a more satisfactory account of coherent behaviour and provide a new perspective on the role of results. We shall begin by reviewing some of these basic theoretical notions.

Servo-mechanisms and Feedback Control

A servo-mechanism is essentially a machine which is controlled by the consequences of its own behaviour. The ingredients of such a device are a source of power, a transducer, which is activated by the power source, a sensing device which measures the output or activity of the machine and a feedback loop which translates the output measure into a signal which can control the input. In Figure 1 the transducer is an electric motor supplied through a device which can vary the power supply and hence the motor speed. The output of the motor used to move a load is measured. This can be done using only a tiny fraction of the actual power output, for instance by attaching a small generator to the output shaft. In this specific instance the small amount of power from the generator could be used to move the setting of a control on the power supply to the main motor. It can be arranged

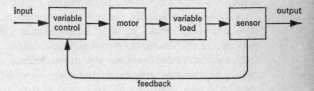

Figure 1　A simple servo

that an increase in motor speed turns down the control, reducing the power supply and slowing down the motor, and that if the motor gets too slow more, rather than less, power is supplied. In this way the motor tends to run at a constant speed despite variations in load. Watt used the same principle in a mechanically operated device to control the rate of the newly invented steam engine, and this was called Watt's governor. Note that, disregarding the Heath Robinson construction of the device shown in Figure 1, there are some important design features to be considered if it is to work properly. The most important of these is the design of the feedback loop, that is to say how information about the motor output is turned into appropriate instructions to the power supply control and the relationship beween power supply control and motor speed. A badly designed servo may 'hunt' to and fro about the desired speed or may go out of control altogether. In very general terms, the designer has to discover the appropriate *transformation rule*, that is to say the means of converting a measure of output into appropriate control action. Given that an appropriate rule can be found (and it usually can although some designs are in principle unstable), a feedback-controlled system has the property of maintaining a set level of output regardless of fluctuations in the 'load' imposed by the environment. Watt's steam engines, for example, were subject to variations in load, but with the governor could maintain a uniform speed.

Although the history of servo-mechanisms is quite long, the principles and applications were advanced rapidly during the Second World War, and in 1948 Norbert Wiener's book *Cybernetics* showed the general relevance of servo-theory to biology and to neurophysiology and psychology in particular. The basic characteristic of maintaining a uniform output despite variations in load conditions presents an obvious parallel with living organisms which, by and large, manage to maintain themselves, at least through the normal life span, against changing environmental conditions.

In 1932, W. B. Cannon in his book *The Wisdom of the Body* had in fact anticipated Wiener by demonstrating some of the elaborate control mechanisms by which the body maintains a more or less stable equilibrium in its internal environment. Yet again, as Weiner pointed out, the ability of the arm, hand and fingers to pick up and move loads as different as a heavy lump of lead and an egg demonstrates the existence of a servo-control system using the feedback coming via both exteroceptors and proprioceptors in the joints and muscles themselves, a discovery made by Bell (1826). When the feedback loop of a servomechanism is interrupted or the transformation rule is changed, the equilibrium of the system is disrupted. Wiener cited the case of *tabes dorsalis*, a disease, which, in effect, blocks proprioceptive feedback from the limbs. In such cases voluntary movement of the affected limbs becomes virtually uncontrollable. The blindfold subject is unable, for instance, to point in a given direction not because he cannot move his muscles but simply because he does not know where his limb is. Acts such as pointing and picking things up become possible when visual feedback is available, but movements tend to be jerky and ineffective.

Clear evidence of the importance of feedback in the performance of basic perceptual-motor skills comes from experiments in which normal exteroceptive feedback is distorted or delayed. Stratton (1896, 1897), for example, used spectacles with lenses which inverted the retinal image. This simple change in the feedback transformation rule severely disrupted the normal process of moving about the world, although after a longish period of practice the subject could manage fairly well. Stratton's original intention of finding out if one could learn 'to see the world the right way up' is not important in the present context.

Some ingenious experiments by Held and his co-workers (see a review by Held, 1965) demonstrate that the effects of spatial displacement of the visual field, induced by wearing prism goggles, can only be overcome by active practice. In a variety of tasks subjects performed simple reaching and pointing movements before, during and after wearing prismatic lenses which displaced the visual field to one side. After wearing these lenses the subjects' pointing errors showed evidence of compensation, that is displacement of movement in the direction opposite to the displacement induced by the prism, but this only occurred when subjects had seen the results of self-produced movement whilst wearing the lenses. In one experimental task, subjects were either allowed to walk about wearing prisms or were wheeled about on a trolley over similar routes for similar times. Subjects who moved voluntarily achieved full adaptation after several hours but the subjects who had been passively wheeled about did not. In short, adaptation to displacements of the visual field depends on the reception of feedback from self-produced movement. The equivalent stimulation from passive movement is not, of course, feedback since it does not depend on any output, so these demonstrations show the importance of feedback as such to the process of adaptation.

Lee's (1950, 1951) demonstrations showed that even the well-practised activity of speaking is disrupted by delaying normal auditory feedback. The subject wore padded earphones which excluded external sounds and spoke into a microphone. His voice was recorded on a tape recorder and played back using a second playback head displaced slightly from the recording head, so that he heard his own speech only after a short delay. With a delay of as little as half a second, speech production was affected. Speech was slowed down, even slurred, and there was a tendency to increase intensity and pitch and a kind of stuttering was often observed.

K. U. Smith in a series of books and articles (see especially Smith, 1962, and Smith and Smith, 1962) has explored in detail a wide variety of transformations of feedback and their effects on motor tasks. Small angular displacements of the visual field are only marginally disruptive to voluntary movement and subjects soon adapt but inversions and reversals are much more disruptive and adaptation takes much longer. Delays of either auditory or visual feedback (the latter achieved by the use of television cameras and video-tape recorders) appear to be the most disruptive of all, and there is little or no adaptation even with prolonged practice. This important difference between displacement and delay is not too difficult to understand in the light of the properties of servo-mechanisms and the kinds of servo-control found in living organisms. A servo can be easily designed to adjust its output according to the magnitude of perceived error. This happens whenever we reach or point to anything. However, if a servo is thus dependent on feedback and we do not have an 'open loop' system which produces a motor output regardless of the result, then nothing useful can be done *until that feedback arrives*. Thus any lag in the system will impose a limitation on performance which cannot be overcome unless some way is found of reducing the lag or of predicting future feedback. This fundamental limitation applies equally to electro-mechanical and biological servos.

Plans and Operations

In the preceding sections we have seen how information about the consequences of an output can be fed back to control further output and we have looked at some instances of servo-control. It is not difficult to find instances of feedback loops in the behaviour of organisms, but, more importantly, behaviour *as a whole* is capable of description in terms of hierarchies of feedback loops. Developing the ideas which have been current amongst engineering psychologists for the previous two decades, Miller, Galanter and Pribram (1960) set about a systematic description

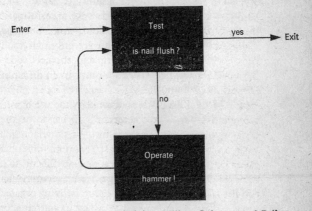

Figure 2   A TOTE *unit (after Miller, Galanter and Pribram, 1960)*

on a behaviour unit called a TOTE. TOTE is an acronym for *T*est *O*perate *T*est *E*xit. The *T*est is essentially an inspection of sensory data which detects any incongruity between the desired and the actual state of affairs. When an incongruity is detected action is initiated (*O*perate) and a further *T*est is made. The cycle continues until the incongruity disappears and the activity is then switched off (*E*xit). The authors' diagram of hammering a nail flush illustrates a recurrent TOTE cycle (Figure 2).

By entering with the arrow at the top left of the Figure we come to a perceptual function, a test of whether the nail is flush or not. If it is we simply exit by the arrow to the right. The 'non-flush' condition leads to the activity of hammering and a further test. Two particularly interesting things about this small segment of behaviour are that it is flexible and it always achieves an objective. It is flexible in the sense that any amount of hammering or none at all may be involved, and it achieves its objective however much hammering is needed. This is the kind of behaviour we expect from a servo system.

Miller *et al.* suggest that the operation of hammering a nail can be taken as evidence of the existence of a *plan* (for hammering nails). As we can see, this particular plan does not deal with certain contingencies such as the nail or the hammer breaking, or the operator getting tired. This difficulty can be overcome by increasing the variety of tests or by linking together more T O T E units in a hierarchical structure as in Figure 3.

This figure constitutes a more elaborate plan for ham-

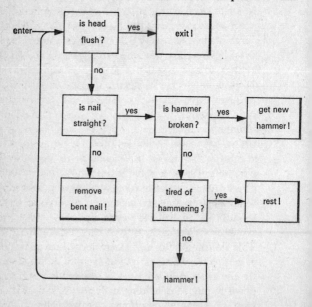

Figure 3   Expanded T O T E *unit for hammering nails*

mering a nail which takes into account a few more possibilities. Again entering at the top left, if the nail does not pass the 'flush' test it is tested again for straightness, and if it is not straight another action is called for. The hammer too is tested and the test has been put in for the operator as well. Note that at least five different activities can result from this series of tests, depending on their outcomes: further hammering, removing bent nails, getting a new hammer, going on to the next task or just plain giving up. This wide range of activities is all essentially feedback-controlled, and illustrates the flexibility of hierarchical feedback systems. In fact if something went wrong with the feedback loops the whole behaviour would become disrupted, and nothing would be achieved.

Descriptions of behavioural plans laid out in this way are now generally known as *algorithms*, and they have been used with considerable success in describing the activities a person must engage in to achieve a given objective (Lewis, Horabin and Gane, 1967). Thus, for example, Duncan (in press) has recently described an algorithm for diagnosing faults in an acid-distillation plant. The algorithm specifies the order in which tests should be made on various parts of the plant depending on the outcome of previous tests. It leads inexorably to the final location of the fault in a minimum average time and at a minimal average cost.

The exit points in the nail hammering example all lead to other TOTE units. In extending the algorithm in this way, we can look at subordinate and superordinate plans. The hammering operation may be part of an overall plan detailing the necessary operations in making, say, a dog kennel. We might have begun by asking 'Is there a dog kennel?', if 'Yes' exit, if 'No', then 'Make a dog kennel'. This is turn would be broken down into sub-operations of getting the wood, cutting it, assembling parts and so on. At the most detailed level of description we might get down to plans for holding nails and striking with a hammer. This way of describing behaviour has considerable promise in analysing practical training and human engineering problems in industry. If overall performance is inadequate one could begin, as Annett and Duncan (1967) suggest, by trying to draw up a detailed plan of the operation to see what has gone wrong. The task is broken down into its constituent operations, each operation being essentially a T O T E unit consisting of an 'error signal' (an input), an activity which should correct the error, and a feedback term which indicates that the operation or sub-operation is successfully complete.

Take, for example, the operation of baking a cake. The sub-operations may consist of preparing and weighing ingredients, mixing and beating, and baking in the oven. Each of these is readily broken down further. Mixing may have to be done in a prescribed order (butter and sugar, egg then flour, and the egg will first have to be beaten and the flour sifted). Few cooks will get *all* the sub-operations wrong. Mary's cakes may turn out sad because one operation has not been correctly carried out. The notorious instruction 'beat to a creamy consistency' may fail because Mary did not know what a 'creamy consistency' looked like. The test phase of the T O T E has failed. By analysing a task in this way it is possible to identify causes of failure in the overall task and apply appropriate remedies.

Human subjects, even after a great deal of practice, do not always have efficient plans. In fact Duncan found this to be so in the acid-distillation problem referred to above. After investigating the task requirements he was able to work out an optimal plan and, quite simply, gave it to the operators in book form, after which performance improved so dramatically that one trainee of a few weeks' standing, who happened to be present in the control room, not only noticed that there was a fault but had correctly diagnosed its source before the shift manager had realized what was happening.

Plans for Changing Plans

We have already shown how T O T E units can be stacked or nested into a hierarchical structure and this is usually necessary when describing behaviour of any complexity. When a control system involves such a hierarchy it can become an *adaptive* control system. The author is indebted to Pask (1961) for the following illustration of adaptive control involving a simple hierarchy. Imagine a busy executive with a secretary. The executive wishes to do his work efficiently and this entails having a regular flow of files, visitors and telephone calls. The pressure of work in the office is somewhat irregular, but the secretary by storing files, asking visitors to wait, and making appointments, etc., can regulate the flow of work to her boss. Both the secretary and the executive are sensitive to the main variable, the flow of work as it affects them, but they respond to it in different ways. If the flow of work becomes excessive, the secretary stores files and puts off visitors as best she may, but the boss responds to the excessive flow of work by sacking the secretary and putting another in her place. If he is a little more benevolent, he may improve the secretarial problem by adjusting the way the secretary works. Both systems, however, boil down to much the same thing and both are instances of adaptive control. At the top of the hierarchy we have a master controller to whom one or more sub-controllers are subordinate. When the output from a sub-controller exceeds desirable limits an alternative sub-controller is switched in by the master controller, or alternatively the transformation rule of the sub-controller is changed. Given that a variety of sub-controllers is available or that the sub-controller can be adjusted, the system as a whole will adapt to the demands of its environment. Such a system does not possess any memory store, only the current setting of its control loops, but it nevertheless exhibits a primitive form of trial-and-error learning. If, following Miller, Galanter and Pribram, we think of the feedback unit describing the master controller as representing a plan, an adaptive control system can be said to have a plan for changing plans.

Knowledge of Results

We have seen how, at a very general level, the concept of feedback can be applied to the analysis of behaviour ranging from the simplest of movements to complex problem-solving tasks. A piece of behaviour can result in muscular and other bodily sensations and changes in the externally perceived environment, including, of course, the social environment. The general term used since about the turn of the century for a variety of forms of psychological feedback is knowledge of results (KR). In this section we will take a preliminary look at some of the types of feedback or KR which can be found in the experimental literature. In general, *intrinsic* KR is that which is normally present and is not often subject to experimenter manipulation, whilst *extrinsic* KR represents feedback being supplied by the experimenter or specially adapted by him. Movements of the skeletal musculature always involve at least two sets of muscles, one set contracting and the other opposing the contraction. A system of reciprocal innervation is necessary if any such movement is to be carried out smoothly and efficiently, and this involves an inter-muscular feedback loop. This basic level of feedback is intrinsic to the movement, it operates at a sub-cortical level and is not readily susceptible to manipulation. At the next higher level, receptors in the musculature and joints register movement and are sensitive to the forces resisting movement, for instance, the weight of the limb itself, and friction, inertia, etc., associated with any object being moved. This feedback is normally *intrinsic*, but it is subject to experimental manipulation which could take the form of varying the forces resisting the movement.

At the next higher level, exteroceptors come into play. For example, in a steering task the subject can not only feel but see the effects of his actual movement, and the performance is directed to some target which is represented visually but not kinaesthetically. Such visual feedback is, of course, intrinsic to the steering task, but it is nevertheless subject to experimental manipulation – by using distorting lenses, mirrors, closed-circuit television, video-tape recorders, and so on. When the experimenter adds an additional feedback loop this may be called *extrinsic* KR or *augmented feedback*. The most common example is the addition of information regarding the standard of performance.

In a tracking task the subject has intrinsic, proprioceptive KR and intrinsic KR of target motion. The experimenter may augment this by adding a time-on-target score or statements such as 'you are doing well' which are not a normal or necessary consequence of doing the task. Much of the research on KR concerns this type of extrinsic KR which is added to and subsequently removed from the task. The distinction between intrinsic and extrinsic KR is worth underlining, even if only to make it clear that many so-called no-KR conditions (where the experimenter stops giving the subject his scores) still leave most of the feedback loops intact. When KR is used as a training technique it is normally present for the training period only, after which the trainee must rely on intrinsic KR. Thus a major question is how extrinsic KR can be used to facilitate transfer to standard conditions where intrinsic KR only is available.

Figure 4 is a simplified version of Fitts' (1962) conception of the feedback loops involved in performance. In this case the system includes a machine which might itself have one or more feedback loops and the social environment is represented by an observer-experimenter who can add extrinsic KR to the normal display or via some other channel.

Feedback loop 1 represents central control of perceptual mechanisms which is probably involved in attention. Feedback loop 2 represents proprioceptive stimuli, and feedback loop 3 represents inter- and intra-muscular feedback. Feedback loop 4 represents feedback intrinsic to the task of controlling this particular machine, and feedback loop 5 represents additional augmented feedback provided by the observer-experimenter presented with the same display through loop 6. Note that whilst the motor system moves the control and the control moves the machine, the machine may also have an effect on the controls and motor system. Loops 7 and 8 represent the resistive forces opposing correction control movements.

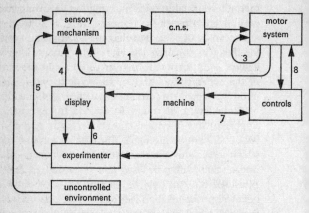

Figure 4   Varieties of feedback (adapted from Fitts, 1962)

In the experiments of the type we shall be describing throughout this book, K R can take a variety of forms, depending on the task and the intention of the experimenter. We shall not, except incidentally, be discussing intrinsic feedback, but we are primarily concerned with extrinsic or augmented K R – that is to say, cases where the experimenter takes some performance measure which is not normally available to the subject and feeds this information to him (loop 5 in Figure 4). The experimental types of K R may often refer to only one aspect of the response. In the positioning tasks we shall discuss in the next chapter, the measure is normally the extent of movement but not its duration rate or acceleration pattern. Next, the selected aspect of performance is usually transformed in some way. Although the subject gets intrinsic kinaesthetic sensations, the extent of movement may be given to him verbally as so many units of length, degrees of arc, etc. Numerical representations of performance indices are, of course, common outside the laboratory in running times on the track, production figures in the factory and examination scores in the school.

The possible transformations are many, and we shall meet these in later sections, but most involve some temporal delay between the response and K R. Many performances can be divided into discrete chunks, and even when the delay in checking the score and passing it on to the subject is no more than that involved in the reaction time of the experimenter, and/or the scoring system, and that of the subject, the information does arrive *after* completion of the relevant response. R. B. Miller (1953) made an important but ill-named distinction between *action feedback* and *learning feedback*. The latter always refers to K R which comes *after* the completion of the response such that information cannot be used to control the response being measured but can only be used by the subject for subsequent responses. Action feedback on the other hand is any feedback which arrives and can be used *during* a response. The distinction is not quite the same as that between intrinsic and extrinsic K R, although in practice there is intrinsic K R associated with the response and extrinsic K R is often given after. There are exceptions when K R which is natural to the task can be delayed, and it is also possible for the experimenter to provide augmented feedback during the course of the response, for example, by giving a running commentary on performance. So far we have been discussing the consequences of action in the contemporary terminology of feedback and information. We now turn to the classical views of behavioural consequences as rewards and punishments.

Rewarding and Punishing Consequences – the Theory of Reinforcement

Although the concept of feedback has come into general use only in the past two decades, psychologists as far back as Bain (1868) and Spencer (1872) have been particularly interested in certain classes of behavioural consequences, namely *rewards* and *punishments*. The role of reward is the strengthening or *reinforcement* of behaviour whilst punishment weakens it. Reinforcement theory views learning as an adaptation to the exigencies of the real world such that behaviour is adapted or modified by the beneficial and detrimental effects of individual responses, or more precisely the *immediately* beneficial and detrimental effect. Just as evolutionary theory proposes that species are subject to natural selection, so reinforcement theory proposes that behaviour is subject to selection by results. Just as evolutionary theory explains the ultimate survival of species in terms of the actual survival of individuals, so reinforcement theory attempts to explain existing behaviour patterns in terms of the survival of responses which have been immediately rewarded. The idea that behaviour is preserved by good effects and altered by bad effects is extremely compelling, but has proved difficult to work out in detail. One difficulty is the gap which often seems to exist between what is *good for* the organism in the sense of maintaining health and well-being and what it *likes* and will seek. Initial attempts to formulate a reinforcement theory arose out of hedonistic philosophies and concentrated on the effects of pleasant and unpleasant results. Spencer, for example, attributed learning to the pleasurable sensations arising from responses initially emitted in a random fashion, and Bain held a similar theory. Both speculated that the pleasurable sensations in some way channelled nervous activity such that those responses with pleasurable results were more likely to be repeated. These early views are summarized and reviewed by Cason (1932) and Postman (1947), but it was E. L. Thorndike who formulated a systematic learning theory which attributed the selection of behaviour to the consequences or effects of action.

Whereas Spencer and Bain had both thought of behaviour in terms of movements, Thorndike's conception was in terms of stimulus-response $(S \rightarrow R)$ connexions which could be strengthened or weakened.

At a man lives and learns, his reaction or response to the same situation or state of affairs changes. Whereas the question 'What is the cube-root of sixty-four?' evoked a response of silent indifference or 'I don't know' or 'What does it mean?', it later evokes a prompt response of 'Four'. We may say that a connexion has been formed between *'cube-root of sixty-four and four'* (Thorndike, 1931, 1966 edn, p. 4).

Learning is a process of changing the strength of these connexions and of acquiring new connexions. Thorndike was principally concerned with two possible reasons for the strengthening or reinforcement of these connexions: the frequency of repetition might strengthen the connexion – the Law of Exercise; and the after-effects might strengthen the connexion – the Law of Effect. The commonsense notion that practice makes perfect makes the Law of Exercise an attractive notion, but Thorndike produced a great deal of evidence (1931, 1932, 1933a and b) to show that repetition alone did not strengthen connexions and that some positive after-effect was required. The two kinds of after-effects are, of course, rewards and punishments, but in fact it turned out to be rather difficult to attach precise meanings to these terms. In his original statement, Thorndike spoke of 'satisfaction' and 'discomfort'.

Of several responses made to the same situation, those which are accompanied or closely followed by satisfaction to the animal will, other things being equal, be more firmly connected with the situation, so that, when it recurs, they will be more likely to recur; those which are accompanied or closely followed by discomfort to the animal will, other things being equal, have their connexions with that situation weakened, so that, when it recurs, they will be less likely to occur. The greater the satisfaction or discomfort, the greater the strengthening or weakening of the bond (Thorndike, 1911, p. 244).

The difficulty with terms such as pleasure, satisfaction, discomfort, annoyance and the like is that they are descriptive of subjective states, but this difficulty was circumvented by offering behavioural definitions. Satisfiers were those things the organism tended 'to seek or do nothing to avoid', and annoyers were those things the organism tended 'to avoid or do nothing to seek'. In his experiments on human learning, Thorndike used almost exclusively the spoken words 'right' and 'wrong' or occasionally small sums of money as respectively positive and negative reinforcers. In his later versions of the Law of Effect, particularly with reference to his long series of investigations of human learning, the magnitude of reward played little or no part, and the effects of annoyers were no longer regarded as equal and opposite to the effects of satisfiers. The result 'right' following a correct paired-associate item was assumed to trigger off an *'O.K. reaction'*, an internal response which was directly responsible for the reinforcement process. The invention of the O.K. reaction, which can be triggered off by a variety of satisfying circumstances is convenient in so far as it gets rid of the awkward gap which exists between reinforcing stimuli and the actual physiological needs of the organism.

The point which Thorndike stressed and the point which seems to be a major source of dissatisfaction amongst his critics is that the function of reinforcers is *automatic and inevitable*. He conceived of reinforcement as a biological process and offered a speculative physiological explanation. 'A neurone modifies the intimacy of its synapses so as to keep intimate those by whose intimacy its other life-processes are formed and to weaken the intimacy of those whereby its other life-processes are hindered. ... The learning of an animal is an instinct of its neurones' (Thorndike, 1931, 1966 edn, p. 59).

It was, however, behavioural evidence which strengthened his view of the automatic and inevitable nature of reinforcement, rather than any experimental confirmation of the physiological hypothesis. This evidence comes out strongly from a large number of experiments demonstrating that people learn only when they receive K R 'right' or 'wrong' but is especially underlined by a phenomenon called the *spread of effect*. Thorndike (1933a) produced evidence to show that not only were correct responses strengthened by the result 'yes', but that nearby responses punished with 'no' were also slightly reinforced. The apparently indiscriminate nature of the spread of effect was consistent with what Thorndike expected of a 'biological' force acting in a direct and irresistible but somewhat haphazard fashion.

Primary and Secondary Reinforcement

The concept of reinforcement was taken up and extended by C. L. Hull (1951). Primary reinforcers reduce primary drives, the basic nutritional and reproductive needs of the organism. Hull attempted to build his theory on reinforcers which were literally 'good for' the organism.

Despite numerous experiments, the neural mechanism of drive reduction remained just as obscure as it was to Thorndike, and Hull's behaviour system could not work without the concept of *secondary reinforcement*. Secondary reinforcement was introduced as an amendment to the principle of primary reinforcement such that stimuli *closely associated with primary drive reduction* can acquire reinforcing characteristics. Pavlov (1927) had already described experiments by Frolov in which a stimulus (a black square) consistently associated with a food reinforcement could itself acquire reinforcing characteristics. The strength of this 'higher order conditioning' as Pavlov called it was, however, weak. Stronger evidence that neutral objects can acquire reinforcing characteristics was demonstrated by Cowles (1937) who taught chimpanzees to obtain food rewards by inserting poker chips into a vending machine. The poker chips were later used successfully as reinforcers in other learning experiments. This is taken as evidence that objects, substances and events which originally seem unconnected with primary needs can be reinforcing, if indeed such evidence is needed, since if the principle of reinforcement is applicable to human learning, almost all the effective reinforcers are secondary, and evidence that animals can also be taught by secondary reinforcers adds little to the argument. In fact it has proved just about impossible to work out the detailed aetiology of secondary reinforcement in humans for various reasons, some practical and some more fundamental. The practical reasons are fairly obvious and might be overcome by determined experimenters prepared either to spend a lifetime in observing the detailed behaviour of young children or prepared to submit babies to tightly controlled experiments. The fundamental problems, however, are that when we get beyond the nutritional needs and possibly sex, we have no way of clearly distinguishing between primary and acquired drives. For the student of human learning the pursuit of the distinction between primary and secondary reinforcement seems doomed to failure.

Strong and Weak Definitions of Reinforcement

The problem of attempting to define reinforcers either as drive-reducing agents or stimuli associated with drive reduction is eschewed by one of the most influential theorists, B. F. Skinner (1953). The alternative he adopts is to define reinforcers empirically. 'Good', a pat on the head, a salary cheque and many other things are empirically reinforcing, and we do not need to know (although we are permitted to speculate) how they came to be so. Skinner sees the progress of experimental psychology as that of relating behaviour to antecedent conditions such as previous reinforcements, not as an attempt to explain how reinforcement works in the physiological sense of primary drive reduction. Skinner's postion on reinforcement is, therefore, closer to that of Thorndike who accepted certain events as empirically reinforcing without requiring physiological details.

This empirical use of reinforcement is referred to as the 'weak' theory of reinforcement in contrast with the Hullian type of 'strong' theory which attempts to account for reinforcement effects in terms of drive reduction. In this context it is perhaps worth mentioning that there are theories of reinforcement which do not involve drive reduction. Guthrie (1935), for example, proposed that the attainment of a reward or the solution of a problem, reinforced the immediately preceding behaviour by virtue of the fact that it removed the subject from the situation. The consequence of his removal from the situation is that stimuli associated with the task are also removed and cannot therefore become associated with other responses. On the next occasion the stimuli occur, they will elicit the responses with which they were last associated.

In a different way, Tolman (1938) also rejected the drive-reduction hypothesis of reinforcement. Some of the experiments which led him to this conclusion will be discussed later. He nevertheless gave some significance to rewards and punishments as 'strong' stimuli which served to emphasize certain consequences. Learning, he argued, consists of building up 'expectancies' which can be understood as hypotheses about what will follow from a response. If something fairly dramatic by way of reward or punishment follows a response, expectancies will be built up rapidly by this added emphasis.

Incentives

Reinforcement is not the only property attributed to rewards and punishments – they are sometimes spoken of as *incentives*. Whereas reinforcers are said to *reduce* drive, incentives appear to *increase* drive. There is a great deal of empirical evidence to show that both animals and people work harder when there is a reward at the end or seek more vigorously to escape from punishing situations. In monotonous and fatiguing tasks the provision of rewards of various kinds is often found to increase effort and energy expenditure and to raise standards of performance. In short, rewards and punishments appear to affect performance as well as learning. Stimuli used as reinforcers can also act as incentives, and often the two functions are hard to disentangle. It could be argued that many of the reinforcers used in animal experiments increase drive rather than reduce it. A pellet of food is hardly likely to satisfy a rat that has been without food for twenty-four hours, but it will make him work hard for more pellets of food. In fact, reinforcers are typically not very satisfying.

The distinction between incentives and reinforcers is none too clear, but if one can be made, it is on the basis of the dependent variable of interest in any given experiment. When more or less permanent changes in behaviour are being examined, rewards are regarded as reinforcers, but when the behavioural change is in terms of energy expenditure rather than a change in response and when the change is relatively transitory, incentive seems the better word. However it would be unwise to assume that the two effects are unrelated and they will both be discussed in detail in chapters 5 and 6.

Concluding Comment

This chapter has been a rapid sketch of the various ways in which the consequences of behaviour are seen to have significance.

The feedback concept is significant not simply because it suggests analogies between organisms and machines but because it suggests certain basic characteristics of the structure of behaviour. Rather than being simply run off as a result of prior stimulation, behaviour, both simple and complex, can be seen as governed by results *at all levels*. In a very general way the feedback concept seems to be able to account for some of the complexities of behaviour and especially with flexible and adaptive behaviour.

The feedback concept was antedated by a variety of

notions that rewards and punishments were primarily responsible for changes in behaviour. Reinforcement theory has taken many forms, few of which we have been able to discuss in detail, but in general they appeal to the notion of drive reduction.

Controversies over various versions of reinforcement theory have been fought out primarily in the field of animal behaviour, but the theory has been applied, by analogy, to knowledge of results in human learning. Reinforcement theorists hold that K R is a secondary reinforcer since it is not always obvious what primary drives are being reduced by the provision of a score derived from a performance measure. Rewards and punishments also have incentive effects, inducing greater effort and apparently increasing motivation. Incentive properties have also been attributed to K R. Knowledge of results as a demonstrable form of feedback has at various times been credited with all three functions, the informative function of feedback and the reinforcing function and incentive function of reward and punishment.

Cautious textbook writers assert that K R has all three properties but decline to say how they are mixed or how they can be disentangled. Others, less cautious, have stuck out for strictly 'informational' or strictly 'motivational' interpretation of K R. Here the central issue is seen to be the separation of informational and motivational effects or the reduction of one to the other. The principal aim of this book is to re-examine this issue in the light of some of the more important findings on knowledge of results.

It is necessary to make some kind of division of the very extensive research literature so for the next three chapters we shall look at motor, perceptual and verbal tasks in turn. These divisions are somewhat arbitrary, but it is necessary to clarify what is meant by such a general term as K R in specific situations before attempting the main task of teasing out the theoretical issues in chapters 5, 6 and 7.

2 Motor Tasks

Positioning Tasks

Discrete positioning tasks have been used by a long line of experimenters on KR. The basic task consists of a number of discrete learning trails. On each trial S makes a single blind movement or excursion from a point of origin, stops and returns. The extent of movement is measured against a standard criterion and KR is given. Learning is normally measured in terms of the increase in movement accuracy. The history of the task goes back at least as far as Woodworth's (1899) *Psychological Monograph*, 'On the accuracy of voluntary movement', and the same basic experiment provides most of the data in a recent review by I. McD. Bilodeau (1966). It was Thorndike (1931, 1932) who had worked with Woodworth thirty years earlier who established 'the line-drawing experiment' as a vehicle for research on learning. It is still possible to design informative experiments with the simple materials used by Thorndike, but recently much of the work has been done with lever-pulling, knob-rotation and bar-pressing which may have some advantages for both recording and, on occasions, transforming the results, and at the same time offering opportunities for varying the resistive forces opposing the movement (friction, inertia and damping).

Elwell and Grindley (1938) had their subjects move two handles to position a spot of light on a screen. The light would be switched off for the non-KR conditions. Bilodeau (1953) used a micrometer with the knob protruding through a screen. Many others like Battig (1954) used a lever and Annett (1959) used a rigid metal bar with strain gauges attached to measure the slight bending when pressure was applied to the free end of the bar.

The discrete positioning task in one (or occasionally

two) dimensions can be regarded as a simplified form of tracking task, although it is most improbable that Thorndike looked at it in this way. The task as he describes it (1931) consisted of a stimulus (s), which is the actual instruction to produce, say, a four-inch line, a response, the four-inch line or a line of any other length, which is taken to be a different response, and a reinforcing stimulus, normally the words 'good' or 'bad', but occasionally a monetary reward. It is, of course, the hypothetical connexion between the stimulus (s) and the response (r) which is said to be subject to reinforcement. As Thorndike saw it, learning was the strengthening of this hypothetical connexion. Thorndike's view is represented in Figure 5.

Figure 5   s–r connexion before (a) and after (b) reinforcement of R₃

The connexions between s *and* R_1 ... R_n are initially random, but following the reward of R_3 the stimulus is more likely to elicit that particular response. However, this description implies a rather too simple view of the nature of positioning responses. In most positioning tasks the response is a graded series of muscular contractions under continuous feedback control. Consider an alternative way of looking at the task based on an analysis by Bilodeau (1966). In Figure 6, s is the signal to produce the movement (r). At the end of r the movement is terminated by intrinsic feedback (I F), and after a short delay the subject is given extrinsic feedback or knowledge of results (K R). After a further delay, a second attempt is made. The introduction of I F at the end of r signifies the important relationship between intrinsic and extrinsic K R, since any given response can only be terminated by I F, whilst the extrinsic K R can only affect the next response, or possibly the use the subject makes of I F associated with the next response. It is, however, possible that for very rapid movements, intrinsic feedback is not so important. Woodworth (1899) distinguished between ballistic and controlled movements. It takes time for proprioceptive or exteroceptive information about a movement to be fed back to the subject. It is possible that some movements

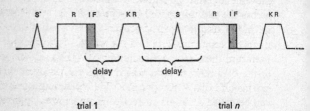

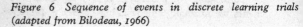

trial 1   trial *n*

Figure 6 Sequence of events in discrete learning trials (adapted from Bilodeau, 1966)

begun and completed rapidly may not be subject to feedback control. Woodworth showed that hand movements completed within half a second are just as accurate when the subject is blindfold as when he has his eyes open and can see his hand.

It seems likely that there may be a class of pure responses in the sense that they depend on some kind of starting signal but not on extrinsic feedback. Of course, Woodworth's experiment rules out visual control only. Kinaesthetic reaction time is known to be considerably faster than visual reaction time and, as far as the present author knows, the experiment has not been done with the anaesthetized arm. However a more sophisticated approach by Taylor and Birmingham (1948) does suggest the possibility of pure ballistic movement in the sense that the response can be pre-planned and triggered off by an appropriate signal. The subject's display was a small spot of light on an oscilloscope screen suddenly displaced a few inches. The subject had to re-centre the light by moving a control stick. The position, the rate of change of position and the acceleration of the control stick were recorded, revealing a complex pattern of accelerations and decelerations. With the possible exception of the final phase the latencies of these bursts of activity are too short to be under feedback control. Thus it would appear that there is some justification for talking about 'the response' for quick corrective movements, and Thorndike's 'quick shove' of the pencil across the pad might well have been of this kind, virtually devoid of usable intrinsic feedback and totally dependent upon experimenter-supplied K R. However, in most of the literature there is no special emphasis on speed, and most of the data refer to tasks which contain both intrinsic and extrinsic feedback components. The positioning task then can be called a simple corrective movement as opposed to the continuous (or possibly intermittent) corrective movements we normally call tracking. There is evidence that, provided the extent of the error to be corrected is in some sense 'known' to the subject, an appropriate pattern of movement including acceleration and braking forces can be generated, and that the execution of this movement is not dependent on either intrinsic or extrinsic feedback. At the same time, since the objective of the movement is correction of error, it is a normal part of such a response that both intrinsic and extrinsic feedback are required and are usually used to control secondary corrective movements until error is reduced to some acceptable level. The characteristics of the classical line-drawing experiment is that the initial error value is not previously known (i.e. the subject has no absolute standard when first asked to produce a line four inches long), and that feedback information comes in two parts, (a) intrinsic feedback, and (b) extrinsic feedback (K R), which comes after the main response and can only be used to correct the next movement.

This raises the rather important general point, that whereas the main theoretical emphasis, from Thorndike on, was on the retrospective significance of extrinsic feedback on the response just made, i.e. the supposed reinforcement of the connexion between S and R, the information may be regarded as telling the subject something about what he must do *next time*. Referring back to Bilodeau's helpful diagram of events we can see quite clearly that K R comes not simply after a response but between responses and, as we shall later see, this factor has some theoretical significance.

The provision of some form of extrinsic K R has generally resulted in at least some temporary learning. The essential fact is that subjects progressively produce lines (or pulls, pushes or twists) which approximate more closely to the standard length or force or angle required by the experimenter. It is necessary, however, to make a clear distinction between the error on a given trial, as measured by the experimenter, and the error information provided to the subject in K R. Bilodeau has made the point nicely by referring to K R provided to the subject as a *transformation* of the error signal or experimenter's response measure. Even the measure taken by the experimenter is of course only a transformation or mapping of the subject's response referring to certain types of outcome of the response, and this is only a description of the response itself in a limited sense.

Much of the history of K R research concerns the type of transformations used and their effects. Thorndike, for example, as a result of his theoretical position on the nature of learning in which reinforcement was intimately associated with notions of reward and punishment, generally used the simple transformation of the spoken words 'good' and 'bad'. His approach was to define the correct response at some arbitrary level of accuracy and to run experiments in which it would be shown that without K R there was no change in the frequency of responses within the criterion category, whilst with K R there was a general increase in the frequency of responses within the required category and a corresponding decrease in 'bad' responses.

In this type of task, unlike many verbal learning tasks, it is possible to attach some meaning to the question '*how* good' or '*how* bad' was the response. This was pointed out by Trowbridge and Cason (1932), and many experimenters not only record this information (as did Thorndike) but also feed it back to the subject. Numerical information in real units like inches or arbitrary units such as 'glubs' does not, of course, rule out evaluative information but rather leaves the definition of what is 'good' or 'bad' to the subject. Numerical information does, however, include the direction as well as the magnitude of error, which is not included in the 'good–bad' dichotomy and this, as Trowbridge and Cason showed, is an important factor in learning to draw a line of given length.

The line drawing/positioning task is well suited to investigations of the general question of how much information is given in KR – a question which we shall explore in a later section.

Positioning tasks have been frequently used in attempts to establish general laws of learning and the effects of KR. Thorndike, for example, showed that mere repetition of a hand movement to the instruction 'move four inches' did not result in improvement unless practice was corrected (Thorndike, 1931). This finding has been challenged, for example by Seashore and Bavelas (1941) who, on re-examining some of Thorndike's data, found indications that successive responses became more consistent although there was no general trend towards the prescribed target length. This raises the general problem of what we are to take as evidence of learning. Thorndike's approach was to look at changes in frequency of 'correct' responses as defined within arbitrary limits, but a more straightforward approach is to look at the mean linear or angular error on successive trials and to plot a learning curve. This approach recognizes that responses admit to degrees of 'goodness' and 'badness', and that a 'wrong' response may still be nearer the required distance than some earlier response. This is now the general approach taken. For example, Annett (1959) in an unpublished study found that average error declined exponentially as a function of the number of trials, and that the shape of the curve did not vary dramatically with different degrees of accuracy in K R, with K R reported in terms of three, seven or sixty categories including, of course, directional information. The group learning curves were virtually asymptotic after three trials with K R.

Inter-trial consistency can be taken as an index of learning, but is not used as the primary index. Where results are arranged over blocks of trials, quite wild oscillations about the target distance could produce a respectably small average error. Clearly the data themselves dictate whether or not variability is a relevant dependent variable. A measure of variability can however become a prime dependent variable in the 'no-K R' condition either during training or on subsequent retention trials. Without the repeated external standard of K R, it could be argued that subjects can show evidence of learning to their own criterion, that is to say, hitting on some response they take to be as accurate as they can make without outside help; they then attempt to repeat this response and get better and better at it. The findings of Seashore and Bavelas mentioned earlier suggest this is at least a plausible possibility.

Bilodeau (1966) has recently proposed consistency as a primary measure of retention in post-K R trials. The retention of positioning responses has, in general, received much less attention than the acquisition of these responses. This is a point of considerable practical importance for training military and industrial tasks, since training with K R, provided by some device, may not be helpful if the task is such that performance will deteriorate to something near its original level when training is terminated. Just this seems to have happened in some of the wartime uses of flexible gunnery trainers, as we shall see later.

Before we leave positioning tasks, one important alternative to distance or angular rotation as a response measure should be mentioned.

Distance simply measures the end point of the response, not how it is achieved. As Taylor and Birmingham (1948) have shown, such responses, particularly when they are ballistic, are better described in terms of time-varying force patterns. Very few investigators have used these patterns as the dependent variable for a learning study and yet it seems obvious that they should be so used. In a much-quoted industrial experiment by Lindhal (1945), trainees were taught to use a foot control on a cutting machine by being shown kymographic records of good and bad cutting movements, and this procedure was reported to be effective. However, there seem to have been no laboratory studies of the effects of various kinds of KR on the time-force patterns of short ballistic movements. Such studies might give some clue to the learning mechanism, whether, for example, KR modifies the movement plan or whether learning takes place by better discrimination of the intrinsic KR.

Tracking Tasks

Although it has been pointed out that the discrete positioning task can be regarded as a sub-class of tracking, there are both practical and theoretical grounds for distinguishing between them. In the tracking tasks discussed in this section, the discrepancy between desired and actual position (of the limb, control handle or target indicator) varies continuously or, at least, in frequent successive steps. Research on tracking has recently been well summarized by Poulton (1966), but for the present purposes a simple description will suffice. A distinction is commonly made between pursuit and compensatory tracking. In pursuit tracking, the subject has a target or target representation, often a spot of light on an oscilloscope screen and on the same screen, a second spot or cursor, linked in some way to a control stick or handle. The target spot moves and the subject attempts to keep his cursor as near as possible to the target by moving the stick. In compensatory tracking, on the other hand, the discrepancy between target and cursor is represented by a single moving light, which the subject tries to keep stationary at some fixed point marked on the screen. Pointing a gun at a moving target is a simple example of pursuit tracking, whilst keeping the speedometer of a car on thirty m.p.h. despite variations in road conditions is an instance of compensatory tracking. The distinction is particularly worth making in the present context because the difference between pursuit and compensatory tracking lies entirely in the way in which error feedback is represented to the subject; indeed the variety of ways in which feedback information can be manipulated in tracking tasks makes them an excellent vehicle for research. In continuous tracking, the subject does not, as a rule, attempt to repeat identical movements as in step tracking or positioning tasks, but tries to respond with whatever movement is appropriate to the size and direction of the error at the moment, or in some cases in the immediate or even relatively distant future. Thus, if learning takes place it cannot readily be described as *learning to make a response* or even a limited number of responses but rather as *learning to process information*. The classic S–R formulation does not fit these continuous tasks too easily, and engineering psychologists, whose particular province this is, prefer to use the language of feedback and information.

Intrinsic KR in Tracking

Referring back to Bilodeau's diagram of the events in positioning tasks, we noted that the feedback is split into two components, intrinsic feedback (usually kinaesthetic) closely associated with the response, arriving with it or immediately after it, and experimenter-supplied or augmented feedback (what is usually called KR) some time later. In continuous tracking tasks the intrinsic feedback, both proprioceptive and exteroceptive, is continuously available and is normally delayed by no longer than the normal reaction time. Whereas it makes sense to try to draw a four-inch line without visual feedback, a gunner could hardly track a target without watching it. This is not to say that blind tracking of a simple input function, for instance a slow sine wave, is not possible nor that the error signal may not be auditory. The point is simply that most tracking tasks consist of apparently continuous corrections to an observable error whilst the blind positioning tasks can be regarded as successive attempts to correct an error which has only become known after the attempt.

In general, then, it would be true to say that in continuous tracking tasks intrinsic feedback is normally present in kinds and amounts adequate for the performance of the task. In so far as an error signal on the oscilloscope normally corresponds pretty closely to the experimenter's measure of error, it is usually possible for the subject not only to track but to improve his performance without the aid of additional feedback. Real-life tracking tasks, involving motor cars, aeroplanes and submarines, have complex dynamic properties such that intrinsic exteroceptive feedback is usually transformed in some way. Measures such as road-speed, altitude and so on, which the subject is trying to control, are usually represented on dials, and this representation is rather different in kind from the factor being controlled. Furthermore, the actual response, such as pulling a lever or turning a handle, may be related in some arbitrary way to the displayed error. Consider, for example, the difference between the caveman who feels cold and throws an extra log on the fire and modern man who reads the temperature on his thermometer and turns a dial on the central heating system. Although the latter is a skill which is very easily acquired, one can envisage the possibility of mis-reading the thermometer or of turning the dial in the wrong direction. These possibilities for error are multiplied many times when the machine system is complex, as when the subject is controlling a chemical distillation plant or steering a submarine. These transformations of intrinsic K R are thus of some importance in the study of tracking behaviour.

In the kinds of complex situation just mentioned an important form of transformation is the introduction of a time-lag between control action and the desired result. Chemical plant and submarines do not respond immediately to control action, neither for that matter do central heating systems. Lag or delay of K R is therefore a fairly common feature and has some dramatic consequences.

The work summarized by Smith (1962), referred to in the previous chapter, amply confirms the disruptive effects of delaying intrinsic feedback in tracking and similar tasks.

Before leaving the topic of transformations of intrinsic feedback it might be mentioned that engineers and psychologists working together have developed the means of overcoming the worst effects of control lags in complex systems. The difficulty with compensatory control is that the helmsman has no means of distinguishing between error resulting from target movement and error introduced by his own responses. All error is summed into a single indicator. Even when actual target motion is quite simple the control lag may allow the helmsman to make a gross over-correction before he sees he has gone too far. From this point on, he is likely to be tracking principally his own error. The technique of *quickening*, described by Birmingham and Taylor (1954), has the effect of giving advance information on the behaviour of the controlled element such that an otherwise unstable system becomes relatively easy to handle. Another more recent system devised by Kelley (1960) generates a special predictor display which shows not only what the controlled element is doing now but what it will be doing in five or ten seconds' time if no further correction is introduced. Both these systems, quickening and the predictor display, can be regarded as a means of giving immediate knowledge of results. A detailed discussion is beyond the scope of the present book and the reader is referred to standard works on human engineering, e.g. Morgan *et al.* (1963).

Most of the work relevant to knowledge of results in the conventional sense has been carried out on tracking tasks with fairly straightforward spatial and temporal relationships between control and error or target display. With suitable apparatus it is possible to manipulate either exteroceptive feedback or proprioceptive feedback and the relationship between these two are, as in the simple positioning tasks, quite important. Variations in exteroceptive feedback can include either the addition or subtraction of information. Thus an additional error indicator can be added to the visual indicator, or the visual indicator can be rounded, or made intermittent, or degraded by noise. Proprioceptive feedback can be varied by adding resistive forces, friction, damping, inertia, to the control or even by anaesthetizing the limb.

Extrinsic K R in Tracking

Additions to the standard exteroceptive feedback have been fairly widely studied in the context of gunnery training. In a typical case a trainee gunner tracking a moving film of an attacking aeroplane must be correct in azimuth and elevation and, in addition, turn a knob which encircles the target aircraft with a variable diameter ring to make an adjustment for range. When all this is done he can pull the trigger and hope to score a hit. In some versions of the S A M Trainer a red filter would drop over the projector and the target image would turn red for a hit. This provides an intermittent form of additional knowledge of results.

An even earlier study by Biel, Brown and Gottsdanker (1944) of the 40 mm gun with a computing gunsight included training in which an expert observer follows a duplicate of the trainee's sight and sounds a buzzer when the trainee is on target. Both these devices were reported successful, but later studies (e.g. Morin and Gagné, 1951) suggested that these improvements had been relatively temporary, and that the gain due to the red filter or check-sight and buzzer techniques did not long outlast their removal. (See also studies by Seashore, Underwood, Berks and Houston (1949) and by Stockbridge and Chambers (1958).) The precise nature of these effects is a little difficult to evaluate in the military setting in which they were originally found. Any attempt to provide a training scheme for the extremely dangerous job of flexible gunnery was no doubt welcome and officers and N.C.O.s administering the training may possibly have supplied their own input of enthusiasm to the results.

More recently there has been a number of laboratory studies of augmented feedback in tracking and these have been particularly concerned with relations between intrinsic and augmented feedback and, in most cases, with retention as well as learning. Lincoln (1954) used a special form of compensatory tracking. Subjects were required to turn a crank handle at a constant specified rate under various conditions involving different types of error information. Error in this case is, of course, deviation from the required rate of cranking. Some subjects were given the information on a dial whilst tracking, and others were given a verbal summary error score after each 15-second trial. Error information was also variously scaled in terms of a standard 100 r.p.m. or 160 ft per minute or 1900 inches per minute or 4800 cm per minute. There were 5 preliminary trials with no K R, followed by 15 trials with one of the K R conditions, 10 criterion trials without K R, and 10 relearning trials. The results tend to confirm the doubts raised by some of the earlier gunnery studies about the value of augmented feedback when it comes to transfer to the criterion (no K R) task. The visual indicator gave the steepest acquisition curve but subjects given only verbal K R soon reached a comparable level. During criterion trials, however, the group with visual feedback was poorer than those with only verbal K R, and Lincoln is led to the conclusion that the visual indicator is too good in the sense that subjects attended to it during the learning trials to the detriment of attending to the intrinsic kinaesthetic feedback. Those subjects without the visual indicator were, therefore, in a rather better position to learn something about the feel of the correct rate which was all they could rely on in the criterion trials.

In a follow-up study, Lincoln (1956) looked at various ways of getting subjects to make better use of intrinsic kinaesthetic feedback. The task was essentially the same and, as before, both learning and retention were tested. Three K R conditions were used. In the first, subjects were given their average error in feet per minute in the immediately preceding fifteen-second trial during inter-trial rest pauses. In the second, subjects grasped the crank which was automatically rotated at a rate equivalent to their average error rate in the previous trial, whilst in the third condition, subjects passively grasped the crank whilst it was rotated at the correct rate. This kind of third condition is not, strictly speaking, a means of giving error information but is logically (if not practically) equivalent to a range of training techniques generally known as *guidance* in which the subject is passively put through the correct responses. Although the guided, standard rate group showed initially more rapid acquisition, there was little improvement beyond the first ten learning trials out of a total of thirty, and verbal K R ended up with better performance, with the second group, direct kinaesthetic presentation of error, in second place. All groups maintained a fair degree of accuracy on the criterion trials.

Karlin (1960) and Karlin and Mortimer (1961) also used a cranking compensatory task to study the learning and transfer effects of different types of feedback. They used no less than thirteen different conditions, consisting of various combinations of visual and auditory indicators, kinaesthetic, verbal, and an instructional lecture. The central point here which comes from the Lincoln study is the distribution of attention to various sources of feedback information. One other feature of the experiment was that some of the feedback was provided intermittently, that is, for the first five seconds and last five seconds of a fifteen-second period. This is a possible technique for giving the subject the benefit of extra information yet having him attend to the essential intrinsic cues for at least part of he time.

In another study, Smode (1958) provided two types of supplementary feedback information to the cues already available, in a visual compensatory tracking task. A high-information group was given an auditory click after each half second on target and a visual cumulative time-on-target score which could be examined between trials. The low-information group was given only time-on-target over a ninety-second target period. After eleven training trials the groups swopped treatments. The high-information group was superior throughout, but transfer to low information resulted in a drop in performance whilst changing from low to high gave an increase. It would seem that tracking is improvable by adding what might be thought to be redundant information to the intrinsic feedback. Transferring from high to low information leaves, within the limits of the experiment, some residual effect. Smode himself suggests that these effects are primarily motivational and by that he seems to mean that the high-information treatment tends to induce greater attention to accuracy or a higher level of aspiration.

Reaction Time

In positioning tasks the performance criterion usually involves using some measure of the accuracy of performance. In tracking both speed and accuracy contribute to scores such as time-on-target and root-mean-square error. Reaction-time tasks are those in which time alone is the criterion variable. Errors, such as pressing the wrong key in a choice task or anticipating the signal, are normally kept to a minimum and seldom feature in criterion performance. Needless to say, the aim of a reaction-time experiment is not that the subject should produce a response of a specified latency but simply that responses should be 'as fast as possible'. This distinction is important in so far as a subject being trained is not being asked to produce a specified response so much as a response with a specification 'better than *x*'. This is also true of ergographic studies and, indeed, in any task where there is, theoretically, no upper limit to the attainable performance level. For this reason KR in reaction-time tasks is often regarded as an incentive rather than as a reinforcer in the strict sense of making a connexion between S and R more probable.

The literature on the effects of KR on reaction time is relatively small. The best known study is by Johanson (1922) who used three subjects and obtained about 1200 simple reaction-time measures from each in a 'normal' condition, an incentive condition, which consisted simply of telling subjects their previous response time just before the next new stimulus, and a third condition in which the subjects got an electric shock through the response key for reaction times in excess of a specified standard. The modal reaction time was about 145 milliseconds for the normal condition and for the KR condition about 130 milliseconds. Electric shock punishment reduced it still further to about 115 milliseconds.

A few subsequent investigators have confirmed the finding that the provision of KR reduced simple reaction time. That this is an incentive effect rather than a reinforcing effect – the latter implying some semi-permanent change as a function of the number of trials of practice – emerges from recent investigations by Church and his associates (Church, 1962; Church and Camp, 1965; and Church, Millward and Miller, 1963). Church (1962) used a competitive situation with subjects working in pairs, each subject trying to get a faster time on each trial than his competitor. Actual times were not signalled to subjects, as in Johanson's study, but a light showing which of the pair had won was illuminated. Compared with a control, non-competitive condition, reaction times were faster, but the increased speed was immediately apparent at the *com-*

mencement of the competitive trials. Church argues that whilst the kind of K R given *could* result in the differential reinforcement of fast responses, the reinforcement process should develop gradually trial by trial. The immediate, sustained improvement does not follow this pattern and so supports the distinction between a reinforcement or learning effect and an incentive effect. The point is substantiated in subsequent work (Church and Camp, 1965) in which subjects competed against their own previous scores. Using a criterion speed based on previous performance, a green light flashed if R T was better than criterion and a red light flashed if R T was worse. There were two control conditions, one with no lights and one with both lights used irrespective of performance. As a sub-condition some subjects underwent trials with a fixed warning interval and others with a variable warning interval. The fixed warning interval is something which subjects could learn and it appears that they did. There was a significant practice effect with K R which was greater for the fixed warning interval condition. However, as before, the effect of K R was pretty much confined to those trials on which it was given. Thus both learning and incentive effects have been demonstrated, and there are some grounds for distinguishing between the two.

We can begin to ask what the nature of this incentive effect is. In the context of simple psychophysical tasks, such as reaction time and including detection and discrimination tasks, it appears that subjects are considerably influenced by what they understand is expected of them. In detection tasks, for example, the subject may be asked to press a key when he sees a change in illumination or hears a sound. He can be instructed that it is important not to miss any signals or he can be told that false positive responses ('Yes', when there is in fact no signal) should be avoided. The former instruction could be regarded as an incentive to detect (i.e. to make the 'Yes' response). Increasing the detection rate in fact increases the false positive rate in a way predictable by signal-detection theory.

Annett (1966a) has argued that similar conditions obtain in reaction-time experiments. The normal instructions to respond as fast as possible and yet to avoid anticipations are, in a sense, ambiguous. Just as a higher rate of detection can be traded off against the increased risk of false positives, so also can reduced reaction-time be traded off against the risk of anticipations. The general instructions are ambiguous if the subject is not told what the trade-off, or rate of exchange, is. What is normally implied by these instructions is shown in Figure 7.

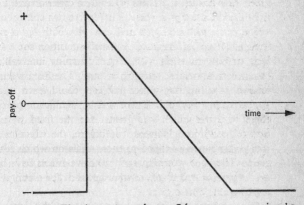

Figure 7   The time course of pay-off for a response to signal s

A penalty, in this case fixed, is imposed for anticipations. The highest positive score is obtained by a response at the first distinguishable instant following the stimulus, or, for the more traditionally minded who assume a minimum of 100 milliseconds for a true reaction time, 100 milliseconds after the stimulus. From this time on, credit is reduced as some function of time elapsed until, after the longest acceptable reaction time, a fixed penalty is awarded which might include discharging the subject from the experiment. It is quite a simple matter to use a numerical score and so define for the subject exactly what he should do with the resources available to him to maximize his pay-off over a given number of trials. The assumption is made that subjects can be persuaded to go for the highest possible score, and this, despite some exceptions, is probably a fair assumption. But subjects can only do this if they are given knowledge of results. If, for example, a given response is an anticipation with a large penalty, the subsequent responses might be adjusted to be a little slower. On the other hand, if S has been getting low positive scores he may try to speed up his reaction time to a point where the cost of anticipation becomes prohibitive. The latter case is probably more common, possibly because experimenters stress the undesirability of anticipations. The so-called incentive effect, then, is not so much *caused* by K R as *mediated* by it. The majority of volunteer or paid subjects want to 'do well', if only they knew what constitutes 'doing well'. In practice, K R treatments such as those described earlier amount to telling the subject that, despite what was said in the verbal instruction, it is worth risking some anticipation to get faster responses. Unfortunately it has been the practice to discard anticipations from the data on the assumption that R T is mediated by physiological processes which cannot take zero or negative time. This seems to be missing an important point about the nature of psychological experiments. These measures are probably more related to decision processes going on both before and after the measured response than to the physiological aspects of the response.

This point of view, for the time being, must be considered speculative. Whilst it brings reaction-time work into line with recent developments in other branches of psychophysics, there has, as yet, been very little investigation of pay-off on reaction time. The finding that K R gives faster reactions is only the starting point. We need to know a good deal more about the effects of pay-off and in particular the trade-off between speed and anticipation. If it turns out that there is a parallel with detection and false positives, our understanding of the results of reaction-time work may well be significantly changed. With respect to the supposed incentive effects of K R on R T, it is suggested that it is not K R in itself which is motivating. If the motivation, in the sense of the desire to do well, is there already, then K R provides the subject with the means of achieving that aim. However, we shall return to this question in chapter 5.

Complex Motor Tasks

Whilst the experimental psychologist working in the field of skills may feel able to reduce almost any essentially motor task to positioning, tracking or speed reaction, real life skills are generally more complex than those studied in the laboratory. Moreover, training involving some form of K R is needed for an increasingly wide variety of tasks. Thus, although much of the theoretically important work has been in the simple tasks mentioned so far, a brief excursion into the real world of complex tasks is desirable.

Since the normal pattern of instruction is first to show or tell the trainee what to do and then, when he has tried, to tell him something about his performance, there is hardly a task for which K R has not been provided in some form or another. Writers on training such as Wolfe (1951), Miller (1953) and Holding (1965) have so stressed the importance of K R that systematically organized training schemes often include some special provision for both recording trainee progress and reporting it back to the trainee. It is not uncommon to use tests for both purposes, and these tests involve specialized equipment, be it only pencil and paper, or in some cases a complex equipment mock-up or simulator (see reviews by Gagné (1954) and Fattu (1960)). The gunnery trainers and simulators already mentioned in the section on tracking fall into this category. English (1942) reported a simple training device to teach the correct pressure to use when aiming a rifle. A small pressure tambour was let into the butt allowing a light to come on when the correct pressure was applied. Stockbridge and Chambers (1958) have also investigated the effects of KR on aiming. In order to facilitate scoring and feedback, equipment can sometimes be modified for use in training. Seymour (1954, 1966) has made extensive use of such devices for giving pressure information in, for example, the correct pressure to be applied or the correct path to follow. Lindahl (1945) attached a kymograph to the foot pedal of a disc-cutting machine and was able to show trainees correct and incorrect patterns of foot pressure.

Such is the prestige of KR as an efficient technique of training that detailed evaluations of such devices are rare, except in some very expensive military trainers. There may be a risk that such elaborate provision is made for KR that the trainee's task is substantially changed, and he finds himself basically engaged in clocking up scores on a register rather than producing, say, nylon stockings or tungsten discs. R. B. Miller (1953) expressed some doubts about some of these procedures.

A practical difficulty in designing a training device with provision for KR is in establishing an appropriate relationship between desirable or undesirable aspects of performance and the actual measure taken and used in KR. In a complex performance a whole variety of factors could lead to measures of success and failure, and it may be difficult to provide the necessary discriminative information. Seashore (1951) hypothesizes that individual styles of performance in common motor skills such as threading needles, assembling nuts and bolts, etc., could very well have developed by the haphazard relationship which exists in real life between methods of performing these tasks and indications of success. This 'work-methods hypothesis' seems plausible and serves to emphasize the practical problem in designing training devices with built-in KR.

The relationship between performance measurement and training is an important one, and the history of maintenance training in the U.S. armed forces is interesting in this respect (Fattu, 1960). In the post-Second World War period increasingly complex weapon systems, such as those connected with air and missile defence, were developed, and at the same time the pool of trained technical staff was depleted by demobilization. The problem was to find men to service this complex hardware and a number of tests of troubleshooting competence were devised. Many of these began as pencil and paper tests and developed into full-size simulators. The scoring facilities required for testing could, in some cases (see Annett, 1965), become available to trainees. Similar patterns of development are seen in the now familiar teaching machines.

Pressey (1926, 1927, 1950) developed a variety of forms of multiple-choice testing devices with the initial aim of grading students. When the devices were so constructed that not only was the student marked right or wrong but he could also see immediately if his answer was correct, the device became a teaching machine. The title of one of Pressey's early papers, 'A machine that tests and teaches', is significant. Tasks involving machinery are often fairly readily adaptable as training devices with provision for KR, but in training for sports the problems are greater since the trainee is most often linked to nothing more complex than, say, a tennis racquet. The coach's debriefing can now be aided by film, however, or, even better, by the use of television and a video-tape recorder which can play back within seconds of the event. The boxer regaining consciousness can now see, in slow motion, the blow that laid him low. The discussion so far has been concerned with the informative aspects of KR. The very fact that complex performance can often only be summarized in some global end score indicating a level of achievement carried with it the implication that KR in complex tasks can more conveniently be used as an incentive than as a source of precise information. In relatively uncontrolled real life situations, it is a practical impossibility to establish exactly how and why KR is working, that is to say whether the main effects can be said to be informational or motivational.

Concluding Comment

Even a superficial look at positioning tasks reveals more complexity than Thorndike envisaged. Except in very rapid responses intrinsic feedback plays a part in terminating the movement, and there is the possibility of an important relationship between intrinsic feedback and extrinsic KR. Clearly KR goes beyond just rewarding and punishing individual responses for it can be shown to have a 'directional' value as well. What constitutes criterion performance is also more complex than it first appears. Extent of movement is the obvious measure, but examination of the consistency of successive movements can reveal a different picture, and the assessment of responses as time-varying force patterns has barely been considered. In tracking tasks intrinsic KR is even more important for without it the task is not possible. Hit scores, time-on-target scores and other measures of performance can be added to the intrinsic KR, but their value is in some doubt in relation to transfer performance. There is a strong suggestion that whilst giving a temporary boost there are no long-lasting effects. Some investigators have regarded the extra KR as having cue value, especially when it is given continuously during performance, whilst others suggest its function is purely motivational. In speed tasks, such as the reaction-time experiment, KR seems to have primarily an incentive effect. It can be argued that the instructions given a subject in a reaction-time task define a system of pay-offs and incentives which are implicit rather than explicit. In motor tasks found in industry and sport, KR is often used in specially designed training devices, but the design of KR requires some care. There is always the danger that the trainee may learn to clock up a good score on the device without learning how to use the KR intrinsic to the real task. In many complex tasks it is doubtful if the effects of information and motivation can be disentangled.

3 Perceptual Skills

Characteristically, in perceptual tasks, the stimulus energy distribution is a major independent variable, responses are generally simple and discrete – for example, 'yes' or 'no' – and the major dependent variable is some measure of co-variation between stimulus and response, such as the probability that a stimulus will elicit a given simple response or that systematic changes in the stimulus value will be reflected in systematic changes in response. In short, tasks we term perceptual generally have to do with detection rates, judgements of identity and judgements of magnitude in relation to carefully specified sets of stimuli. Because we are not assuming that perceptual tasks are different in kind from other types of tasks but only that certain characteristics are stressed, we leave open the question of whether the processes of learning are different. In the period roughly between 1914 and 1945 the distinction between perceptual and motor was sharpened by the fact that, in general, investigators in perception and those working with more clearly motor tasks such as maze-learning or lever-pulling held rather different views of the nature of the learning processes. On the one hand learning could be viewed primarily as a matter of the selection of responses to be attached to a given stimulus, whilst on the other learning was the result of changes in perceptual organization which, according to many workers in this field, followed its own laws. Thus the role of knowledge of results in learning looked very different from these two points of view. In the one view the role of K R was in the selection of responses whatever the superficial nature of the task, whilst in the other, K R was simply another factor in the total stimulus pattern, interacting with others according to the laws of perceptual organization. It is not surprising that perceptual learning was a kind of no man's land between the two major schools of thought, and neither side trespassed very far into this dangerous territory. In recent years, however, interest in perceptual learning has been renewed, partly due to attempts by a newer generation to bridge the gap and partly for the purely practical reason that perceiving is still one of the activities in which human beings maintain their superiority over machines, hence men are given tasks involving detection, discrimination and recognition and have to be trained to perform these tasks.

The field of perceptual learning has recently been reviewed by Epstein (1967). For the present we shall be concerned with a limited selection of research studies on the use of K R in training mature subjects in relatively simple judgemental tasks, leaving out the question of how developing organisms learn to perceive. Eleanor Gibson (1953) has reviewed this area; more specific (auditory) studies have been reviewed by Annett and Clarkson (1964) and Annett and Paterson (1966, 1967).

Detection

In practical terms the simplest form of perceptual task is detection. Normally there is only one stimulus pattern although it may vary in total energy (e.g. a light varying in brightness, a sound in loudness) and a simple response, 'Yes' (signal present) or 'No' (signal absent). The detection problem arises when stimulus energy is not much greater than energy from non-stimulus sources, for example a sinusoidal tone may be embedded in a background of ran-

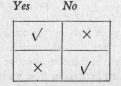

dom white noise. The possibilities are classified in this simple 2 × 2 matrix. It is possible to be right in two ways and wrong in two ways. Stimulus energy, or signal/noise ratio, and also stimulus probability can be independently varied. When stimulus probability is relatively high and stimulus energy is systematically varied, the task establishes what is known traditionally as the *absolute threshold*. When stimulus probability at any particular time is low, the task is usually classified as a vigilance or monitoring task. In this case stimulus energy is often, but not necessarily, held constant at a rather higher level.

The main question now, is, can the proportion of right and wrong responses be changed by practice in which KR is given? Various forms of KR can be used. Each correct detection can be signalled and correct 'no' responses can be confirmed. In addition, S can be told of omissions, that is, 'no' responses in the presence of a real signal; and finally false positive responses can be disconfirmed. This information can be reduced either by giving only one of these measures, say detection, or by giving some kind of combined score – for instance, detection weighted by omissions and/or false positives – or simply by delaying the information until the end of a set of trials. It is important to note that the information given in KR can, in this type of task – unlike, say, line drawing – be given in advance. It is just as easy to tell the subject there will be a signal on the next trial as it is to tell him after his response that he was right or wrong. This technique of giving advance information as an alternative to KR has recently been known as *cuing* and is obviously related to *guidance* or *action feedback* in motor tasks or *prompting* in verbal tasks. The comparability in terms of information given by cuing or KR enables us to explore (for these tasks at least) a general aspect of the properties of KR conceived as a reinforcing agent acting retrospectively on the connexions between a stimulus and a response. If the mechanism of KR is considered only as acting in this retrospective sense as in the classical reinforcement paradigm, then we might be at a loss to explain any training effects resulting from cuing without making some more assumptions. Having set the stage we can now look at some of the experimental results on detection training.

An experiment by Annett (1966b) on the effect of different kinds of K R on the detection of bursts of pure tone masked by white noise illustrates some of the variations of K R and their effects. A control and four training groups were used for nine successive five-minute trials during each of which about twenty signals were given at irregular intervals. Training was given on the second, fourth and sixth trials. One group was given a summary of hits, misses and false positives at the end of each five-minute trial, whilst another group received a light flash, 0·5 seconds after each signal giving equivalent information in close temporal contiguity with the relevant stimulus and response events. In a third condition, the visual signal appeared 0·5 seconds before each tone (direct cuing). This in fact made the tones much easier to detect (see also the work of Howarth and Treisman, 1958) and so a fourth group was trained under easier conditions with the background noise reduced to the point where detections increased to about the same extent as occurred in the cuing group. The control group received no K R and simply practised the standard task for nine trials. The results were compared on the basis of a performance index, a detection score weighted for false positive responses. In the training trials 2, 4 and 6, both the warning light (group III) and the reduced noise (group IV) were dramatically superior. Their task had in fact been made much easier, but whereas reducing the noise had only a temporary effect, a significant part of the gain was retained by the warning light or cuing group during the three post-training trials. Summary K R had no effect on performance, but the immediate K R (light flash) group improved significantly but were still inferior to the cuing group. These results suggest that improvement in detection performance is possible but that not all means of giving K R are effective, and also that the warning signal or cuing technique is, at the very least, as good and probably better than immediate K R.

A number of other investigators have found various forms of K R effective in increasing the detectability of simple auditory signals (Loeb and Dickson, 1961; Lukaszewski and Elliott, 1961; Swets and Sewall, 1963; Zwislocki *et al.*, 1958), although Campbell (1964) failed to find an effect and Swets and Sewall concluded that training effects are small and limited to the early stages of practice.

Campbell's negative result may have been due to the use of a method in which signal intensity was varied according to the current level of performance so as to obtain a uniform detection rate; Swets and Sewall, who found only small effects, used a variety of different signal intensities. It appears also that signal frequency interacts with the ability to profit from K R. Zwislocki *et al.* (1958) found greater improvement with low-frequency signals (125 Hz) than higher frequencies such as 1000 Hz, a finding partially confirmed by Loeb and Dickson (1961). In most cases rapid learning occurs in the very early stages, the first fifty or so trials or the first practice session, and thereafter improvement is very slight.

One of the most striking results is that of Gundy (1961) who, prior to training with K R, presented the signal three times at a much higher intensity than that used during normal testing and training. Following this 'signal specification', further K R had only a marginal effect on detectability. This suggests that what was being learned was something about the characteristics of the signal and this is acquired rather more slowly by using a standard correction or K R procedure. The cuing technique in which a warning signal is used may be having a rather similar effect. Annett and Clarkson (1964) and Annett and Paterson (1966) have found that the warning signal or cuing technique significantly affects sensitivity to the signal. On the other hand, K R by itself has little effect on sensitivity but increases the detection rate by lowering the response criterion. That is to say, K R does increase detection but at the cost of many more 'yes' responses to noise alone. Tentatively, learning to detect a previously unfamiliar signal masked by noise seems to require that the subject builds up a 'template' of the signal characteristics by being given samples of the signal which are identified as such. New instances can then be matched against this template. If the subject only gets the signal specification (i.e. the information that this is a sample of the signal) by making a 'yes' response, it is in his interests to produce a large number of 'detections' and so we get a low response criterion. Annett and Paterson (1966) found some confirmation of this hypothesis by using a short, fixed, observation interval after which S was forced to respond 'Yes' or 'No'. In this case the K R and cuing techniques produced very similar results. It thus appears that the main function of K R is an informative one, that is to tell the subject that this sample of signal-plus-noise can be added to the template against which future samples of signal-plus-noise or noise alone can be compared.

Monitoring Tasks

Some of these experiments would be classified as monitoring studies in so far as signals come at poorly specified intervals and the subject is allowed to respond *ad lib*. When monitoring is over an extended period and the dependent variable is a change in the threshold, normally a decline over that period, then the study becomes one of vigilance. One of the earliest and best known studies of the vigilance decrement was by Mackworth (1950), and the topic has been extensively documented since (see Bergum and Klein, 1961; Broadbent, 1958; Buckner and McGrath, 1963; Frankman and Adams, 1962).

Using a variety of tasks including the monitoring of visual displays on which signals to be detected appeared at infrequent and irregular intervals, Mackworth found a progressive time-dependent decline in detection efficiency. He showed that, in both visual tasks (the clock test) and an auditory task, knowledge of results given verbally by the experimenter after each response or failure to respond was effective in preventing the vigilance decrement. Mackworth proposed a classical conditioning explanation of these phenomena. At the beginning of the experiment the signal to be detected was demonstrated; this he took to be the conditioned stimulus. The instruction to 'Press the response key now' was the unconditioned stimulus resulting in the normal unconditioned response of key pressing. Knowledge of results, 'Yes' or 'Yes, that was right', was the reinforcer and in a few trials the subject is conditioned to produce the key-pressing response. In a long session without K R a process of extinction might take place giving rise to the observed decrement which in turn can be removed by the reintroduction of K R. For a variety of reasons this theory has now been abandoned. K R does not increase the probability of correct response to 1·0, nor, in the absence of K R, does the response extinguish completely.

A number of other theories are current, including one based on operant conditioning (Holland), one on expectancy (Deese) and one on selective filtering (Broadbent), but these will not be discussed here (see Buckner and McGrath, 1963). A theory which is of some interest in the present context and is that of Broadbent and Gregory (1963) who propose that the vigilance decrement is due to a progressive change in response criterion, in the signal-detection theory sense. This is of interest in so far as the Annett and Paterson studies suggest that training with K R is primarily effective in lowering response criterion. It might follow, therefore, that the beneficial effects of K R on the vigilance decrement are due to this factor and, furthermore, that it may be possible to train subjects to adopt a low criterion and hence to resist vigilance decrement. An attempt was made to test the latter hypothesis in a small experiment (Annett and Paterson, 1966). Having produced, as the result of one experiment, two groups of subjects, one having a high criterion and another a low response criterion, these subjects were, after a brief refresher training, required to monitor an auditory display continuing for thirty minutes. Unfortunately, although both groups maintained their relative positions with respect to response criterion, neither changed over the trial period without K R: in short, there was no decrement in either high or low criterion cases. Decrements tend to be less severe in auditory tasks and, in our case, signals were fairly frequent, both of which points may account for the failure to find a decrement. The hypothesis that vigilance decrement is a change in criterion and that K R changes the criterion remains to be thoroughly tested.

Discrimination

In the discrimination task, the subject is normally presented with two stimuli, a standard and a variable, and his response is either to say if there is a difference or to specify the way in which one stimulus differs from another, for example, whether the second of two weights is heavier or lighter than the first. The forced-choice technique is generally to be preferred for methodological reasons. Difference thresholds have been established for a wide range of sensory dimensions, but only a few studies have been concerned with practice and learning. Brown (1910) used a correction method (K R) and found some improvement in weight discrimination but uncorrected practice also yielded some improvement.

In vision there is a considerable body of literature from the animal laboratories, including work by Pavlov, but in human subjects the correction of errors in the visual illusions is of some interest. Judd (1902, 1904) was responsible for early work on the Müller–Lyer illusion and demonstrated that the effects of the illusion were reduced by practice. Some limited K R was available but since the subjects (Judd himself and one other) were aware of the nature of the illusion, including the direction of the judgemental error, the effectiveness of K R *per se* is not too clear.

Other illusions such as the horizontal/vertical illusion (Williams, 1902) and the Poggendorff illusion (Cameron and Steele, 1904, 1905) have produced substantially inconclusive results. Gibson (1953) comments:

These experiments with illusions permit almost no conclusion except that, in many cases, illusions do decrease with practice. Knowledge of results as practice progresses is not essential but the role of the observer's attitude toward the judgement he is making is not clear. Most experimenters were concerned that the decrease in c e [constant error] occurred without any conscious attempt at correction. It might be worth making further studies in which the subject's attitude is carefully controlled and varied, including a series in which *S* is given knowledge of results and instructed to try to compensate for his errors (p. 30).

Due, no doubt, to the practical considerations in musical training and more recently in the training of sonarmen, there has been a number of studies of the effects of training with k r on auditory difference thresholds. Pre-1953 studies are reviewed by Gibson, and recent work by Annett and Paterson (1966 and 1967). Campbell and Small (1963), for example, trained subjects for six sessions, some subjects receiving immediate k r on series 1, 2, 4 and 6 and some only on trials 2, 4 and 6. Whilst there was overall reduction in difference thresholds from first to last, Campbell and Small reported that k r had, if anything, a disruptive effect when given early in practice. The groups having k r from trial 1 remained consistently worse than the group having k r from trial 2 onwards. A study of Heimer and Tatz (1966) compared k r with non-k r training and found that frequency difference thresholds improved equally well for both groups.

In view of this doubt about the effectiveness of k r, Annett and Paterson (1967) carried out yet another investigation on the trainability of the frequency difference threshold. In a two-alternative forced-choice situation, four groups of ten subjects each were compared. Group 1 received immediate K R to a response 'higher' or 'lower' (in pitch) by the use of a punchboard. A second group punched the board one stop ahead thus getting advance information as to whether the variable signal was of higher or lower frequency than the standard. A third group began training by this cuing method and halfway changed to K R on the hypothesis that K R containing too many 'wrongs' in the early stages may be more disruptive than helpful. A fourth group practised without benefit of K R or cue information. Groups 1, 2 and 3 all showed significant improvement over three hours' practice, but there were no significant differences between them. The control group made only a slight but insignificant improvement. A similar finding was obtained with the threshold for intensity differences between two tones. Using the same method for differences in the duration of two short tones, we were unable to find any improvement with practice either with or without K R. Referring back for the moment to the detection experiments, the subjects' willingness to respond (response criterion) was obviously sensitive to K R. With the difference-threshold experiments, however, the use of the forced-choice method meant that subjects had to commit themselves to a response ('higher' or 'lower') and the problem of response criterion was thus eliminated. It is interesting to note that, in these circumstances, the K R and cuing techniques appear to be equivalent. Both provide additional information about the signal at or near the time it is presented. The fact that K R is, strictly speaking, contingent upon the responses does not appear to be of any consequence.

Magnitude Judgements

In detection and discrimination tasks, the number of responses open to a subject is normally very limited, yes or no, more or less. When, however, the subject is required to examine a stimulus and make an estimation of magnitude of some property of the stimulus, such as its size or intensity, the range of possible responses is potentially un-limited, although the subject is sometimes limited by the experimenter to the use of a scale, say numbers 1–10, or 0–100. Perceptual estimation tasks may, therefore, have more in common with the positioning tasks mentioned earlier than with simple detection and discrimination. Subjects may be asked to estimate the length of a line in inches or may be required to classify a line *n* inches long. The difference, if there is one, is that in verbal estimation there is no problem in saying 'three-and-a-half inches' having once decided on the length, whereas the non-symbolic response, 'three-and-a-half inches' made by drawing a line, may be in error.

Although one might wish to make such a distinction between judgemental and response processes it is not, in practice, easy to do so. Thus in verbal estimation procedures, the legitimacy of talking about learning effects in terms of response selection is not easily denied. Some of the earliest experiments in the effects of K R on estimation were carried out at the turn of the century by Thorndike and Woodworth (1901), and some thirty years later Thorndike (1931) published the results of visual/verbal estimation experiments and spoke of them in terms of response selection through the reinforcement supplied by K R. In a typical experiment, subjects are presented with strips of paper of varying length with a standard 10 cm strip always before them. K R was given in the form 'right' or 'wrong' and the subjects generally improved. In this case we see two techniques, the provision of an anchor as well as the provision of K R, and both could have had an effect on improvement. Gibson (1953) concludes from her survey, which includes estimation experiments in a variety of modalities, that 'A combination of anchoring by appropriate presentation of stimuli and defining of response categories, followed by practice with correction which aims at reinforcement and differentiation of discrimination, should be most effective'.

An experiment by Annett (1966b) on the visual estimation of the number of dots presented in a tachistoscopic field illustrates the effect of anchoring and K R. At the beginning of the experiment all subjects were shown a few samples of fields with numbers of dots ranging from ten to fifty. Subjects were then divided randomly into three groups, one of which continued to estimate without K R, a second group was told the correct number of dots after each trial and a third group was told the correct number before each trial. All three groups had therefore been given some anchoring information but group I did not improve beyond the initial trials either in C E or V E. The remaining two groups improved in C E and V E to about the same extent. Had the K R group alone been tested, improvement might have been attributed, in the manner of Thorndike, to the reinforcing effect of K R; but, of course, K R can also be regarded as providing anchor information. The third group could be regarded as having anchor information in some detail throughout training, but since the information they obtained was not contingent upon and did not follow responses it can hardly be regarded as reinforcement. It might therefore be argued that the effect of K R in this type of task is essentially to provide anchoring. This would be all very well if one knew more about the processes underlying anchoring, but they are as obscure as those underlying reinforcement: to explain one in terms of the other is not particularly helpful. On the other hand, the evidence does suggest that perceptual learning can take place without explicit K R and that learning does seem to be greatly assisted by giving the subject frequent pairings of the stimuli to be judged and the appropriate scale values.

Identification and Recognition

Finally we come to a group of perceptual tasks in which the problem is to produce an appropriate name for a stimulus. The stimulus is usually complex, i.e. multi-dimensional, and the name is a category rather than a number indicating a value along one or more of the dimensions of the stimulus; in short, the subject has to identify or recognize the stimulus. Here again we are faced with an enormous range of investigations. It has long been recognized or assumed that motivation plays an important role in perception. Whilst it may be a fair assumption that subjects in general will exhibit 'perceptual defence', for example, taking longer to respond to tachistoscopically exposed 'taboo' words, more rigorous experimental control can be obtained if subjects can be trained to fear previously neutral stimuli. Hence, there has been a number of studies on K R, or, more specifically, reward and punishment on the perception of complex stimuli. A classic example is an experiment by Shafer and Murphy (1943) in which subjects were exposed to the two halves of an ambiguous figure at the same time being rewarded or punished. After the training period, the two halves are recombined into the ambiguous figure and the question is which half is seen as figure and which half as ground? Shafer and Murphy reported that the rewarded profile was most readily seen, but this experiment triggered off a series of replications and variations (reviewed by Epstein, 1967), and there is now considerable doubt about the generality of the original finding. Perhaps the most significant factor in these researches (as with work on verbal conditioning in the next chapter) is that the knowledge of results has, in the main, consisted of attempts to reward, usually with money, or punish (e.g. with electric shock) rather than with giving information in any differential or quantitative sense. The motivation of mature human subjects is rather difficult to control or to be sure of within the range of conditions acceptable to the society in which these experiments are done. In short, the validity of the reinforcer is always in doubt and here the matter must, for the time being, be left.

It remains only to mention some studies of auditory pattern-recognition training. Of particular interest is a series of studies by Swets (1962), and Swets, Harris, McElroy and Rudloe (1964) using computer-assisted instruction. Complex sound signals which could assume any of five different values along any of five dimensions constituted the material to be learned. The sounds were presented by a computer and the subject could enter a five-digit number, the name of the sound, on a teleprinter keyboard. A variety of tuition methods were available and subjects were given some freedom to choose the methods by which to learn. They could, for example, opt for a prompting mode in which the computer typed out the correct answer and then presented the tone, or they could opt for a test mode in which, after they had heard the sound and typed out an answer, the computer could give correct information along any one or all of the individual dimensions. It would also arrange to repeat the sounds or even to play back the sound corresponding to the subject's wrong answer.

The main conclusion from these studies, an interesting one from the point of view of instructional technique, was that the students did not know what was good for them. Relating success to the amount of time spent by the subjects on each of the training modes, the simple prompting technique was found to be most efficient. Many subjects however, tended to spend more time on the less efficient test modes, that is to say, attempting responses and getting various forms of knowledge of results. In view of other results on the effectiveness of cuing and prompting techniques in relation to trial and error, this is again an interesting result. Even though the computer provided KR swiftly, the sounds themselves had gone by the time the correct answer had been typed out. An interesting postscript is provided by Sidley, Winograd and Bedauf (1965), also using complex sounds. In one case, the sounds remained audible during the subject's response and the consequent KR. In another case KR was, as in the Swets studies, provided only after each sound had ended. Improvement in the former case was 45 per cent and in the latter case was only 20 per cent. So once again we find the close temporal contiguity between the stimulus and its 'name' to be a potent factor in these forms of perceptual learning. Close contiguity would facilitate the 'specification' of an ephemeral signal.

To conclude, in a variety of 'perceptual' tasks various forms of K R have been found to be effective. However, under certain experimental conditions an important effect of K R is to increase the subject's readiness to respond rather than to increase sensitivity to the signal as such. With appropriate controls for variation in response criterian K R can be effective but the fact that cuing or signal specification techniques are also effective leads to the conclusion that improved sensitivity as such is due to the information provided in the cue or K R signal and that a classical S–R reinforcement model is not at all appropriate.

4 Verbal Learning

Whilst it seems convenient to deal separately with motor, perceptual and verbal tasks, closer examination makes these distinctions appear arbitrary. Yet tasks do have specific characteristics; particular variables seem more or less important and are more or less easy to manipulate. The verbal tasks we shall be concerned with in this section are the classical serial list and maze learning, paired-associate learning, the type of task now generally known as verbal conditioning, and certain types of concept formation and finally programmed learning which is essentially a practical application and can embrace any or all of the foregoing types.

The fact that responses are vocalized makes these tasks verbal, but this may not be important. Behaviourally, a series of utterances, for example a nonsense syllable list, is hard to distinguish from learning a maze which also encompasses a set of responses, the precise order of which is important. Indeed a maze may be regarded as either a motor, or a perceptual or a verbal task. Learning to associate pairs of words, the first of each pair being presented as the stimulus and the second being the required response, can readily be given a motor parallel where the stimuli are displays of lights and the response to be learned is which key to press. With elaboration on the stimulus side and perhaps some simplification on the response side, such a task could easily be described as a perceptual recognition task. Verbal conditioning tasks are specifically designed to parallel closely simple instrumental conditioning. The responses which are selected and rewarded are verbal but they could just as well be gestures as words. Again, concept learning tasks, whilst normally involving a verbal response, could equally well be manipulative. In many cases the stimuli are patterns for which the subject has to learn to produce the appropriate class names or to state a rule relating sub-classes of stimuli, and the parallel with perceptual recognition is often stressed.

What makes all these tasks verbal is not simply the use of words or letters so much as the fact that either stimuli or responses or both are drawn from the population of behavioural patterns we call language. This is true even of nonsense syllables and from this there follow at least two important implications. The first is that the behaviour under investigation in the experiment is very closely linked with a rich and over-learned repertoire, the effects of which can never be entirely eliminated from the experiment. The second is that language behaviour can be covert, all the necessary stimuli can be self-generated and all the responses to them be kept below the threshold of external observation, so that the observable behaviour can be mediated by a host of unobservable events. This is not to say that manipulative or perceptual tasks are never mediated by symbolic processes (be they linguistic or non-linguistic). Despite all these problems there still would seem to be some value in looking separately at verbal tasks and pointing out the differences between these and non-verbal tasks where they seem to be important.

Serial Learning

Nonsense syllable lists learned by the method of serial anticipation contain entirely adequate intrinsic K R. The response is attempted, the correct item appears giving complete K R and serving as the stimulus to the next response. In this type of task, K R variables are not very readily manipulated. For example, the transformations of K R which are a feature of lever positioning tasks are not readily achieved in the classical serial learning list. Delays in K R can be arranged but since the K R is also the stimulus for the next response, even if it is not the occasion for it, this raises an extra complication. The amount of information in K R can be only crudely manipulated, for example by defocusing the image of the correct response or by supplying only some of the letters. Such manipulations do not fall on a simple dimension like length or angle, and in addition difficulties are created in so far as the K R is again the stimulus for the next response. Leaving the serial learning task as it stands, extrinsic K R or augmented feedback can, however, be added. Russell (1952), for example, gave half the subjects learning a list of twelve nonsense syllables by the serial anticipation method instructions intended to produce high motivation whilst the other half received instructions designed to produce low motivation. Half of each group again were told that they were failing badly whilst the other half received no indication of their performance. All groups learned the list to the same criterion, and retention was tested either one minute later or the next day by the re-learning method. Those under the failure condition showed much poorer retention after one minute, but for those tested a day later no such difference could be found. Clearly this additional kind of K R was not a very significant factor in the learning process. We should not, however, pass over this example too lightly since many practical learning situations are characterized by K R intrinsic to the learning task but with addition K R of the incentive type supplied by the teacher. This can disrupt performance, possibly also stimulate it, but the effect, if we take Russell's result as an example, seems to be rather peripheral to the basic learning process.

In another study of the classical twelve-item nonsense syllable learning list, Buxton and Bakan (1949) compared, amongst other things, correction and non-correction techniques. The standard serial anticipation method was used as a non-correction technique, whilst for correction subjects repeated aloud the correct response after any failure to anticipate. This additional stress on correction did not lead to any noticeable difference in learning over the standard method. In retention there was some evidence in favour of reminiscence, i.e. better performance than at the end of learning, whilst in the non-correction group there was some forgetting, but both these were interaction effects related to a rest condition. All in all then, the classical serial list learning experiment contains its own in-built K R and additional manipulations lead to only marginal effects.

Maze Learning

The maze also has its own intrinsic K R. A correct response is quickly followed by arrival at the next choice point and a wrong response immediately leads to a blind-alley check. However, as with nonsense list learning, there is some scope for varying or augmenting K R. In an extreme case, we can have an essentially open maze in which the subject is left to wander with no correct route specified. Either all routes lead to the goal or none does. In the latter case we have the classic latent learning situation in which only after some practice is a real goal introduced, thus creating right and wrong patterns. In the alternate case where blind alleys are blocked off and the goal or exit is attained by following the only available route, we have another class of experiment which was studied extensively in the 1920s and 1930s especially by Carr (1930) and his co-workers at Chicago with both animal and human subjects. This condition is generally known as *guidance*, and sometimes as teaching or tuition and is rather close to prompting or action feedback (Miller, 1953) techniques in which error is artificially reduced or prevented. Since on guided trials there can be no error, additional K R would be entirely redundant, but guidance is often compared with the free trial-and-error situation where the subject receives feedback telling him whether his responses are right or wrong. Ludgate (1923), for example, literally guided subjects' hands through the maze. Guided trials were given either at the beginning of training or at intermediate stages during learning and two different mazes

were used. In about 25 per cent of the subjects in one of
the mazes, guided trials were completely adequate for
learning, and in most cases guided trials had some value.

Koch (1924) investigated guidance with both human
and animal subjects. He found that it was generally more
effective (compared with trial-and-error learning) with
rats than with humans and that guided trials are more
effective early in training, although a very few guided
trials just prior to mastery are very effective indeed. In
these cases, trial-and-error learning was mixed with guided
learning. Large amounts of guidance could have several
effects. In the first place the subject might lose some of the
motivation to learn since what he has learned is rarely
tested. In the second place, learning something about blind
alleys and wrong responses generally might in some way
be necessary in learning the correct path.

Waters (1930) examined the question of whether large
amounts of guidance really were deleterious to learning.
He compared four groups of subjects, one working on
trial and error, one on twenty guided trials, one on forty
and one on eighty guided trials. The efficiency of guidance can be assessed in two ways, either in terms of the
total number of trials (guided plus unguided) to criterion
or in terms of the number of unguided trials to criterion
following guidance. On the latter criterion the more
guided trials given the less there remains to learn in unguided trials. This is true in terms of trials, errors and
running time. On the other hand, whilst the control (trial-
and-error) group learned in 37·48 trials, the groups having
eighty guided trials still took another 23·4 trials to complete the learning of the maze – i.e. rather more than twice
the number of trials in all. Carr (1930) summarizing a
number of studies from his laboratory concluded that
guidance is more effective than trial-and-error learning,
provided that only relatively small amounts of guidance
are given early in practice.

One of the essential questions in this area is 'how valuable
are errors?' The above finding suggests that the making of

errors, subsequently corrected by K R, is a necessary and desirable part of learning. In the work we have just been discussing, there were more ways of being wrong than being right. Some more recent studies have made use of binary mazes, the advantage of this arrangement being that right and wrong responses are, in the technical sense, equally informative. Kosofski (1952), rather than using manual guidance, arranged a buzzer for either the correct movement or the incorrect response at each choice point. One set of subjects had to learn the maze avoiding the buzzer and another group received the buzzer on every response. The group getting the buzzer for the correct choice was slightly but not significantly superior. This result would be expected where right and wrong responses are equally informative. In another serial maze study, von Wright (1957) used a twelve-unit diamond maze presented on a paper strip which was drawn slowly by a drum past a viewing slit wide enough to show about half of each diamond. Subjects moved a stylus to the left or to the right to indicate the correct arm of the V. In the standard condition, one arm of the inverted V forming the top of the diamond was scored by indicating a blind alley which became visible only after the choice had been made. Subjects attempted to learn the maze by the standard serial anticipation method. Guidance was introduced simply by marking blind alleys on the lower half of the diamond; thus subjects could see the correct path just before entering their choice. In another form, only the correct path through the maze was seen. Subjects under these two conditions were just given the four guided trials and then returned to the standard maze. Guided subjects were very much superior to those learning the standard maze, those under the second condition, with all parts of the maze visible, being the best. This result contrasts strikingly with others on guidance. If we argue that where errors and correct responses are equally informative the first two groups at least should have been roughly equal as Kosofski found. But this is a matter we shall have to take up in more detail in dealing with the informative aspects of guidance and K R in chapter 7.

One final aspect of maze learning is relevant to our present discussion, namely the addition of signals to the intrinsic K R produced by the maze. Rexroad (1926) and Bunch (1928), for example, both administered shock for errors in multiple-choice or maze tasks. Whilst Rexroad found only a slight effect, Bunch found that punished subjects took only about half the number of trials to learn and reduced both time and errors by about one third. Tolman (Tolman, Hall and Bretnall, 1932) used the maze situation with additional rewards and punishments to challenge Thorndike's Law of Effect. These investigations found that an electric shock for a correct response aided learning more than a shock for a wrong response, and that a bell for a correct response was more effective than a bell for a wrong response. The experiment was repeated by Hulin and Katz (1935) using only the bell condition. A marginal advantage was found in four of the bell-for-right group. Gilbert and Crafts (1935), in a rather similar experiment using buzzers, clicks and shocks, found these 'strong' stimuli had an appreciable effect as compared with control conditions; but there was little to choose between them. Since additional stimuli do not add any information to existing intrinsic K R and since the shock is not effective as a punishment in eliminating responses as would be suggested by a simple-minded view of the Law of Effect, Tolman adopted the position that these 'strong' stimuli simply acted as 'emphasizers' and in this way assisted learning. Bernard and Gilbert (1941) in a further experiment seem to strengthen this view. Two groups of subjects learned a stylus maze, each group getting shocks for one half of the cul-de-sacs. Comparing the learning of shocked and non-shocked cul-de-sacs, it was found that the shocks assisted learning, shocked cul-de-sacs being eliminated more rapidly than the non-shocked. Taken with the earlier evidence on correct responses, this strengthens Tolman's position that additional strong stimuli, including punishing stimuli, act as emphasizers. However, he went further, suggesting that a law of emphasis could be substituted for the law of effect.

In serial list and maze learning we may tentatively conclude that the way subjects are permitted to respond and obtain feedback information does have some effect on learning. The evidence on guidance in this respect is somewhat contradictory, but it seems likely that the relative efficiency of guidance has something to do with the kinds and amounts of error information available in the situation. The standard forms of serial learning include intrinsic K R but some effects on learning are obtainable by augmenting K R. The suggestion so far is that the effect is to emphasize the relevant aspects of the task. Just how this effect works remains obscure.

Paired-Associate Learning

In 1931, 1932 and 1933, Thorndike published the results of a very long series of investigations on human learning. Many of the experiments he reported would nowadays be classified as paired-associate learning, although they were often referred to at the time as serial learning. Typically, the subjects were presented with long lists of items (e.g. eighty) at a fairly fast rate and were required to make an arbitrary response, often a two-digit number, to each item. The lists were repeated many times and a single experiment might consist of several thousand presentations. In the classic serial anticipation method described in the previous section, successive items become both K R concerning the previous response and the stimulus for the next. The fact that K R was always given may have led to its being ignored. Indeed none of the earlier workers seem to have entertained the possibility that learning might be due to the intrinsic K R. Thorndike set about the task of demolishing the theory that sheer frequency of repetition was the cause of learning and to set in its place the Law of Effect. He did not, however, look for reinforcers within the serial learning task but redesigned it to introduce them. Thus in many of Thorndike's experiments there is a set of stimuli, to each of which arbitrary responses are initially made and these responses are reinforced (or not) by the experimenter saying 'right' or 'wrong' after each. Unlike the serial list learning in the Ebbinghaus tradition, it is not so much the contents of the lists themselves which are learned as the appropriate response to each item in the list. One of Thorndike's classical experiments may be taken as an example.

Consider the following experiment: An individual supplies letters to complete a list of 160 words like those shown below. He is to write one letter for each dot

bet...	c .. ss	fa ..	dig ....
b .. e	d .. n	f .. e	fl .. t (etc.)

He does this daily or more often until he has written the series from sixteen to twenty-four times including sixteen to twenty-four completions of b . at. ... The situation, write a letter to make b . at into a word, evoked the response of writing *o* in nine out of the first sixteen occurrences (two for each of eight subjects), but by the last sixteen *o* was the response only two times, whereas *l* was the response nine times. As you have doubtless guessed, the consequences attached to writing *o* and *l* were different. By the rules of this particular learning experiment, no letter save *l* was right as a sequence to *b*. When he had written *l* the subject was rewarded by the announcement 'right' by the experimenter. When he wrote *o* he was punished by the announcement 'wrong'. This is a sample of the many cases which may be observed in the laboratory or in life where frequency competes against the consequences of the connecting, and loses (Thorndike, 1931, 1966 edn, pp. 30–31).

Experiments of this sort were conducted by the prolific Thorndike and others in great variety.

Any multiple choice learning which begins with ignorance will serve. For example, subjects learned more or less of a vocabulary of 200 Spanish words arranged ... by choosing a meaning and being told 'right' or 'wrong'. .... Such cases of great strengthening of one connexion compared with another of equal or nearly equal initial strength by reason of the different consequences attached to it and to others can be found by the thousands (Thorndike, 1931, 1966 edn, p. 32).

One can indeed multiply such instances indefinitely and extend them beyond verbal tasks to judgements of size, distance, etc. Yet the Thorndikian task has some characteristics which make it somewhat unusual and, in certain respects, atypical of natural learning situations. In the first place, anyone wanting to memorize a list of spellings or Spanish vocabulary would be very ill-advised to use Thorndike's method which is, to say the least, slow and inefficient. The materials he chose, quite deliberately, represent arbitrary connexions. There are usually several roughly equal possibilities (but not an indefinite number). This was experimentally necessary in order to demonstrate progressive increases in the strength of favoured associations or outcomes over the strength of unfavoured associations. In the usual form of paired-associate learning and in most educational practice, only one response term is ever paired with a given stimulus term. Not only does this reduce the possibility that any wrong association may be accidentally formed, but it also releases the experimenter or the teacher from the task of adding that the given response term is 'right'. If we wish to stick closely to the Law of Effect then we must, as pointed out before, attribute two functions to the response term, its function *qua* response and an additional reinforcing function. That is, it must have in it the characteristic of being right, which must function as a reinforcing event. Whilst this sounds like unnecessarily multiplying entities, it must follow from Thorndike's basic position.

Two other characteristics of the Thorndike experiment are the sheer quantity of materials used in any one experiment and the number of repetitions. It is hard to think of any explicit methodological reason for using lists as long as 160. Typically work in the Ebbinghaus tradition used lists of about twelve items. What we now know about the importance of interference between items was never explicitly acknowledged by Thorndike as a possible factor in his results. The number of repetitions required and the fact that there was a high repetition rate for wrong responses was almost certainly due to the sheer quantity of material used in these experiments.

Given such an atypical learning situation, the subject's attitude towards the material and to instruction was of some importance. Wallach and Henle (1941, 1942), for example, found it comparatively easy to pass off a typical Thorndike experiment as an investigation of ESP in the manner of J. B. Rhine. Arbitrarily pairing words with numbers in a list repeated many times and having the experimenter say 'right' and 'wrong' produced identical reinforcement conditions to those in Thorndike's experiments, but gave the subject no reason for or against repeating the correct responses. It turned out that rewarded responses were repeated in 11·1 per cent of cases and punished responses repeated in 11·8 per cent of cases. Nuttin (1953) has followed a similar line, distinguishing between open and closed tasks. Open tasks, says Nuttin, have a double aspect, the question of success or failure at this item and the matter of progress towards the final task goal. With closed tasks, on the other hand, success or failure on a given item is the end of the matter and it bears no relation to future task requirements. In other words, subjects in the Thorndike or ESP situation can either take each success or failure as indicating something about what is to be done on the next occasion, or they can treat each event as independent. Nuttin, like Wallach and Henle, goes on to produce evidence to show that the open task attitude, on the part of the subjects, is crucial to obtaining results consistent with the Law of Effect. Opinions differ as to whether this point is crucial to the Law of Effect in any of its many forms but discussion may be postponed to a later section.

Verbal Conditioning

We now turn on to a related type of learning task known as verbal conditioning or the conditioning of verbal operants. In the paired-associate tasks we have been discussing in the previous section, the intention is to establish an association between a specified stimulus term and a specified response term, such that given S, R will occur with increasing relative frequency. In operant or instrumental learning tasks, the aim is a little different. The subject in a given situation is producing responses, the stimuli for which are not necessarily known. Responses are selected by the experimenter for reinforcement, and, in a successful experiment, the frequency with which these responses are emitted by the subjects is increased. The method has been firmly established by Skinner as a technique for training animals, where the reinforcement is usually achieved by the provision of food, water or anything else relevant to some basic and urgent need. In the case of human subjects, learning experiments have been conducted in which the behaviour conditioned consists of verbal utterances and the reinforcer is a verbal comment by the experimenter. We are thus dealing not only with verbal learning but verbal reinforcement. Thorndike was convinced that the words 'right' and 'wrong' were, in human learning, completely equivalent in their effects to more substantial rewards and punishments such as food or shock in the case of animals. In recent verbal conditioning work, experimenters have seldom used comments as explicit as 'right' and 'wrong'. The supposed reinforcers are generally rather veiled remarks such as 'uhuh' or 'go–od' or simply a nod of approval. The way this particular game is played is indeed designed to keep the subject in the dark about what is going on and to establish 'learning without awareness' on the part of the subject. A typical experiment is that of Greenspoon (1955). The subject is simply instructed to say all the words he can think of individually, and not in sentences or phrases. The experimenter, who is behind and out of sight of the subject says 'hum-humm' after each plural noun emitted by the subject and nothing else. This goes on for about twenty-five minutes.

For the next twenty-five minutes the experimenter is silent. The number and type of words emitted by the subject in five-minute periods is counted. The general result is that plural nouns are produced more often when reinforcement is present than when it is not and that the rate slowly decreases during the second 'extinction' phase of the experiment. Experiments of this kind have been reviewed by Krasner (1958), Greenspoon (1965), Holtz and Azrin (1966), and by Kanfer (1968). In about 75 per cent of published studies, positive results have been reported, that is to say, some or even most of the subjects have shown a definite tendency to increase the response class which was followed by reinforcement. The results, however, are rather varied and there are several important methodological and theoretical problems. Three main points have to be considered; first the effectiveness of verbal reinforcers, second the problem of awareness, third the representativeness of these experiments.

The experimenter's comments (um-humm, go–od, etc.) are taken to be secondary reinforcers, but, of course, all secondary reinforcers can only be defined in the circular sense that they increase response probability. The published literature indicates only partial effectiveness and unpublished results obtained in laboratory classes over several years indicate a much lower success rate in the region of 10 per cent. All that is meant by 'success' here is that there is evidence of a significant increase in the frequency of reinforced responses, but even in successful experiments reinforced responses seldom occur to the exclusion of all others. For example, in Greenspoon's case, the reinforced plural nouns accounted for only 30 per cent of all responses emitted. For whatever reasons, verbal reinforcement is not a very effective means of controlling behaviour and most rote-learning techniques would aim at a much higher success rate. Producing only 30 per cent correct answers in a multiplication table would not be considered very satisfactory. There are various possible reasons why verbal reinforcers are only partially effective. The relationship and relative status of subject and experimenter are thought to be of some importance, and some variations in results can be attributed to this. It might also be argued that 'um-humm' is only a very mild reinforcer, but it is difficult to conceive the use of stronger reinforcers which would not alter the basic character of the experiment. If a desirably large sum of money or perhaps even a score were used, more subjects might become 'aware' of the reinforcement contingency and this brings us to the second problem.

These experiments, at least when they are successful, are said to demonstrate learning 'without awareness'. If the reinforcement process is characterized by the biological inevitability attributed to it by Thorndike, evidence for learning without awareness is taken to provide important support for reinforcement theory. Awareness can only be defined operationally in terms of a certain pattern of responses to a post-experimental questionnaire. Subjects are deemed to be 'aware' or 'partially aware' to the extent that they can, on careful questioning, state the reinforcement contingency. Lack of awareness does not mean to imply that the subject was in any sense unconscious during the experiment. In this case 'awareness' constitutes some additional verbal behaviour which emerges as a result of the experimenter's manipulations. The strict behaviourist wishes to avoid attributing causal effects to these additional verbal processes, for learning has to be attributed solely to the reinforcement contingency. The fact that changes in behaviour can be brought about without 'awareness' does not, however, prove that concomitant verbal behaviour is in all cases unrelated to the learning process. Clearly if subjects are told 'the aim of the experiment is to induce you to repeat words of the same type as those which are followed by 'um-humm', the result would be quite different. Without being able to offer a detailed analysis of the role of 'awareness' (in the operational sense of concomitant verbal processes such as being able to state the reinforcement rule), it is clear that these processes can be relevant to the efficiency of learning. Strictly speaking the behavourist position *should* be that they are *irrelevant* to learning but this is clearly not the case. By emphasizing that learning can take place without awareness the relevance of awareness is tacitly acknowledged.

Finally we are led to the question of the representativeness of verbal conditioning. The fact that some aspects of verbal behaviour can in certain cases be manipulated in this way cannot be taken as providing us with a unique model for the acquisition of all verbal behaviour. Indeed, the verbal conditioning experiment is a very specialized game played by the subject and the experimenter. It seems to be sensitive to quite minor variations from ideal conditions, and as a teaching technique it is extremely inefficient. There are some analogies between verbal conditioning, concept attainment and programmed learning but, as we shall see in the next two sections, the analogies are of a rather superficial nature.

Concept Learning

The nature of 'concepts' has been discussed by experts in child development, philosophers, cyberneticians and behavioural psychologists from widely different points of view. For the present purpose we are simply discussing a certain class of experiments in which, characteristically, the subject is taught by some form of KR (or reinforcement) to produce a single response to a stimulus set consisting of one or more, sometimes an indefinite number, of distinguishable members. In the simplest form of the concept learning experiment, the subject is presented with an array or series of instances which may be pictures of objects, geometric patterns or even words. Each instance is characterized by a set of attributes, for example, geometrical figures may vary in shape, size, colour, orientation, number of figures, etc. In a simple case, the instances are to be classified into two groups according to their attributes, for example, all red forms, regardless of shape, etc., as against all other-coloured forms. There can, of course, be many more than two categories and the appropriate combination of attributes can be as complex as desired. There can even be attributes present which are not relevant to the sorting rule. In general, one of two procedures is followed. In the first the subject is presented with an array of instances and required to sort them into groups or indicate the group membership of instances in the array (Bruner, Goodnow and Austin, 1956). In the second procedure *E* presents instances serially in a predetermined or random order and asks the subject to assign each instance to one of two categories. The first (sorting) procedure has been used in the form of a test and the subject is not normally told whether his sorting is right or wrong. However, we are concerned with teaching and learning procedures in which the subject is told, normally after each response, whether his guess is correct. Usually the experimenter determines the definition of the concept to be learned.

In the case where instances are presented serially, and especially in the two-category case, we have an experiment similar to the verbal conditioning studies outlined in the previous section. The subject is shown one instance and guesses whether this is an instance of the concept to be learnt. He is then told whether his guess is right or wrong. Both techniques provide K R, but an important difference between them is that, in the former case, the subject is free to select instances. This enables him, in principle at least, to choose instances in such a manner as to maximize the amount of information given in K R. For example, having formed the hypothesis that the concept to be learned is 'all items which are red and have a border', on the basis of previous results with red squares and red triangles he might now choose a red circle rather than, say, a green rhombus. Such procedures on the part of subjects have been described by Bruner as 'strategies', and it is clear that some strategies can be defined as ideal for a given situation or stage in the problem, in the sense that the results of guesses can be maximally informative.

All this is not to say that the sequential presentation prevents the subject, or at least some ideal problem solver, from forming hypotheses and developing guessing strategies, but simply that the operation of hypotheses and strategies is more obvious to the experimenter in the former case, since it is possible to describe patterns of guessing quite objectively. In the serial presentation case, the subject's guessing strategy (if he has one) may not be obvious, and evidence about the hypothesis can only be gained by questioning the subject, a procedure which involves major theoretical and methodological problems.

In explaining concept learning, we can take one of two approaches. We may adopt the conditioning approach which stresses the reinforcement aspect of the knowledge of results, which prefers to avoid using terms like 'hypotheses' and 'strategies' and which tries to account for concept attainment in terms of the gradual conditioning of stimulus attributes to the simple response. Alternatively, we can take a cognitive approach. We can postulate how a rational problem solver (human or machine) could develop hypotheses and guessing strategies, and we can look at knowledge of results in terms of the information it provides. Human subjects in many investigations have been shown to conform, more or less, to both models! The classic example of concept learning in the reinforcement tradition is that of Hull (1920). The material for this experiment was Chinese characters which were made up of smaller elements (radicals). The same radical appeared in a variety of different characters, and Hull drew up a set of 144 cards based on twelve radicals appearing in different characters. The subject's task was to learn to give the same name to all characters including the same radical, there being, of course, twelve names in all. The stimulus cards were presented in batches of twelve, the experimenter supplying the names on the first presentation and the subject being required to learn thereafter by the serial anticipation method. The gradual kind of improvement typical of conditioning was found. Like the later experiments on learning without awareness, subjects were able to do quite well without being able to state the formal classification rule.

In a typical experiment on the formation of a conjunctive concept by Bruner, Goodnow and Austin (1956), the subject is presented with an array of eighty-one cards each carrying one or two or three crosses, squares or circles in one of three colours and surrounded by one, two or three borders. All possible combinations are represented. The experimenter selects the concept to be learned, say 'all cards containing red squares and two borders', and the subject is shown one positive instance and is asked to choose further cards which might belong to the category the experimenter has in mind. After each choice, he is told whether the chosen card is a positive or a negative instance. In this experiment, there are 255 possible ways of grouping instances into conjunctive concepts, and the first card logically eliminates 240 of these. The information given about each card can be described in terms of the number of remaining hypotheses it eliminates. The strategy requiring the full consequences of each choice to be computed Bruner calls 'simultaneous scanning', and most people capable of working out the problem would need pencil and paper. Subjects tend to choose strategies making fewer demands on memory and computational capacities. Successive scanning involves testing only one hypothesis at a time, for instance that 'red' is the common feature. The subject typically tests this by selecting 'red' cards but in doing so, each choice enables him to rule out fewer alternatives. The information in K R is therefore partly redundant. Conservative focusing consists of taking the first positive instance and altering one attribute at a time. For example, if three red circles with two borders is the first positive instance, the subject may next choose two red circles with two borders. If this too happens to be positive, the attribute 'three figures' is ruled out, and so the subject proceeds. This strategy, whilst eliminating much of what Bruner calls 'cognitive strain', at the same time guarantees that feedback will not be totally redundant. On the other hand, it does not guarantee that a given choice will be maximally informative. In the fourth strategy called 'focus gambling', the subject starts from a positive instance and changes two attributes at a time. As its name implies, this strategy involves some risk. For example, if given a positive instance, the subject changes three of the four attributes and his choice is still a positive instance, then he is home and dry. If, on the other hand, the instance turns out to be negative, very little information has been gained.

In the context of knowledge of results, one rather important idea emerges from this analysis. First note that the K R is, as in the case of Thorndike's work, simply 'right' or 'wrong'; yet depending on what move the subject has just made, and indeed why he made it, K R can be more or less informative in the sense of contributing something or nothing to the solution of the problem. The general point, which is so seldom made in relation to K R and which is so clearly pointed out by Bruner's analysis, is that *the informative function of* K R *is not necessarily in the hands of the experimenter alone.* The subject can make responses designed to extract information whether the experimenter says 'right' or 'wrong', and, moreover, the subject can do this efficiently or inefficiently. From the conditioning point of view, the subject's behaviour must be regarded as planless and only shaped by the results taken, as it were, at their face value. From the cognitive point of view, responses (right or wrong) can be a means of extracting information from the experimenter or from the problem he has devised. As we saw in Bruner's case of focus gambling, a negative instance can be much less informative than a positive instance. It is a general finding that subjects have more difficulty dealing with negative instances (or 'wrong' guesses) than they do with positive instances. We may recall the investigations of Thorndike and others on the relative values of reward and punishment on the reinforcement and elimination of responses. The general conclusion was that punishment (negative instances) does not weaken associations by anything like the amount that reward strengthens them. Von Wright's maze experiment seems relevant here. The guided maze, a series of positive instances, was far easier to learn than the maze allowing subjects to make mistakes. Bruner hypothesizes that negative instances which 'infirm' an hypothesis entail cognitive strain. It is not simply that the subject has received a check and may be running out of alternative hypotheses, but that, if he is to make use of the information, he has to remember his previous positive choices. In one experiment the situation was rigged such that one set of subjects chose mainly positive instances and others chose mainly negative instances. The subjects tackled four problems in succession. One of the findings was that subjects receiving positive instances tended to adopt the focus gambling strategy which, you will recall, involves changing more than one attribute at a time and which is very effective if the subject is lucky in getting positive instances. Subjects faced with negative instances went in the opposite direction towards conservative focusing, the strategy involving the least memory load.

Buss and Buss (1956), in a serial presentation task, compared the performance of three groups of subjects who were informed of correct choices only, or of wrong choices only, or given complete right/wrong information. Curiously, negative information only was as effective as the condition with both positive and negative information, and both were more effective than positive information only. This exceptional finding may very well have been due to an artifact since right and wrong instances were not equated for frequency, but this problem will be taken up in a later section. Certainly the matter of negative information is in need of further research.

The information available through K R in concept learning experiments can be subject to other variations. The number of relevant and irrelevant attributes and the number of alternative hypotheses will affect the function of KR. In the special case of probabilistic concepts, where some defining attributes are not always present, negative instances are less informative since they do not necessarily disconfirm the hypothesis. Other manipulations can be made. Bourne and Pendleton (1958) carried out an experiment in which one group of subjects was given the usual right/wrong information and a second group was in addition shown the correct response. As might reasonably be expected the second group did rather better. As in most other learning experiments, KR can be omitted on a proportion of trials, delayed by so many seconds, and indeed subjected to most, but not all, of the transformations found in other fields. In general, the effects of this kind of manipulation on concept learning are consistent with those found elsewhere (Bourne, 1966a and 1966b), but we shall have more to say about this in chapter 7.

Programmed Learning

In chapters 2, 3 and 4 we have been looking at some of the main laboratory tasks in which the effects of knowledge of results have been studied. We end this part of the book on a different note for, although many of the investigations we shall now be discussing were set up primarily as experiments, programmed learning is an attempt to apply laboratory findings to everyday learning situations. The scene of action is not the laboratory but a real school or college, the experimental subjects are students who, in the main, genuinely need to acquire useful skills like spelling or algebra by working with the experimental task. Surely if the results of many years of laboratory work are worth anything, it will be apparent in programmed learning.

✓ It is not very easy to give a precise definition of programmed learning since there are several main species of program each with many variations and each based on different assumptions about the nature of learning and the learning process. What they all have in common can be reduced to a few points.

(1) To qualify as a program in the currently accepted sense, the material presented to the learner must have been carefully arranged along lines suggested by some systematic analysis of the subject matter or skill to be acquired.

(2) The whole process is governed by the empirical rule that the material is adapted to the student population by evaluation and revision. If the program is not an effective teaching instrument in its initial form, then it is revised until the desired standard is achieved.

(3) The program is presented in a tutorial situation designed to teach the student individually with the minimum of instruction by the teacher. Where it can be shown to be advantageous (e.g. in learning team skills) or at the best not disadvantageous, there can be more than one student in the tutorial group, but the principle of individual tuition is almost universal.

(4) Finally, all programming methods emphasize that the student should be active rather than passive in learning and should receive immediate knowledge of results.

For those readers who have not yet come across a program, the essential characteristics are as follows:

Pressey type. Each student has a set of multiple-choice questions, sometimes supported by other material, a lecture, film or text, and a device which automatically scores his answers right or wrong. As an example, a four alternative choice question is answered by pushing a stylus into one of four holes in a board. Wrong answer holes are partly blocked and the stylus can only be pushed home in the right answer hole.

Skinner type. (Often designated as *linear, short step* and *constructed response.*) The material is arranged in a unique teaching order having been broken down into a large number of sequential small steps. Each step is usually no more than a sentence or two from which some key word is omitted. The subject constructs his response by completing the blank. The correct answer is then revealed. Since the steps are small and the sequence carefully arranged subjects are normally right, hence the correct answer provides confirmation or reinforcement of the response.

Crowder type. (Often described as *branching* or *intrinsic*.) Again an ordered presentation of material but in somewhat larger steps, each step ending in an multiple-choice question. On choosing an answer by pressing a button (in the machine form), a new item appears either confirming a correct response and then passing on to the next step or explaining how that particular answer was wrong and directing the student to further remedial material. The term 'intrinsic' indicates that the program sequence is implicit in the possible alternate routes rather than explicit and predetermined.

In all three types frequent and immediate knowledge of results is a central feature. Pressey, for example, stressed that it was the immediate knowledge of results provided by the punchboard and similar devices which turned a mere test into a valuable teaching tool. Skinner went much further, drawing a direct analogy between the reinforcement procedure, in which the behaviour of a hungry animal can be progressively altered (or *shaped*) by the provision of food rewards contingent upon the desired responses, and the immediate confirmation of individual responses made by the human learner to the program material. For this reason a careful analysis is made of the components of the skill or subject matter to be learned, and the learner is induced to make correct responses and these are reinforced by immediate confirmation. In other words, Skinner regards the knowledge of results in programmed

learning as providing immediate reinforcement. By contrast Crowder, whilst admitting that knowledge of results may have a reinforcing component, uses the results
of the multiple-choice tests primarily as a means of diagnosing the learner's weaknesses and so providing appropriate additional information. He sees knowledge of results as equally important to the teacher and the learner
in determining an optimal tutorial interaction by means
of the branching system.

Whilst all three types of programmed learning have been
shown to work successfully there remains a controversy as
to *why* they work. Is knowledge of results in programmed
learning really providing reinforcement as Skinner suggests or is the success of programmed learning due to
other factors such as the way the subject matter is analysed
and presented? We shall now take a look at some of the
research which is relevant to this basic theoretical question.

Pressey (1926, 1927 and 1950) and his associates developed the multiple-choice testing and teaching technique over a number of years and in a variety of forms.
Used traditionally as a technique for automatically scoring
quizzes, the teacher collects his results and passes them on
to the pupils, perhaps in some other form at a later time.
The virtue of the automatic self-scoring device is that not
only does the teacher get the assessment but the pupil gets
it too and knows immediately how he is doing, and moreover where he is wrong. However, to the extent that his
first answer to any question is wrong, he may quickly
discover the correct answer without invalidating his score
sheet. The idea that this speed-up of knowledge of results
is beneficial as compared with traditional tests has been
more than adequately confirmed by Pressey's own results
and those of other investigators. Angell (1949) compared
the two methods just described in teaching university
freshmen and found a definite advatange for the immediate
K R group in a final exam. Michael and Maccoby (1961)
in an elaborate experiment used multiple-choice quizzes
at intervals in a film on civil defence. One group was

given immediate K R in the sense of being told the right answer and another simply answered the questions without K R. The former group turned out to be better, although answering questions without corrective K R was better than simply just watching the film. An interesting minor finding was that students who 'thought' their answers did as well as those who had to write them down.

In a dissenting study Freeman (1959) found no effect, but he used only two fifty-item quizzes in a course lasting a month. He also tried unsuccessfully to trace the effects of reinforced quiz items in the final examination. The balance of results is certainly in favour of the use of automatic immediate K R.

Bryan and Rigney (1956) elaborated the multiple-choice technique by providing not simply knowledge of right and wrong but also some explanatory material. Three groups of forty-eight students did a 150-item test. A control group did the test without K R, a second group received right/wrong information, and a third group selected their answer by pulling off a paper tab which revealed explanatory material. When tested a week later, the third group was significantly the best. This experiment and those just described raises the issue of what is giving the effect. In all these cases which provide a clear-cut result, it would appear that the test was giving the student information he did not previously possess. The reason may have been inattention or simply poor presentation, but whatever the reason these experiments do not clearly distinguish between the hypotheses (1) that learning was due to the immediate reinforcement of correct responses, and (2) that the student was acquiring new information. Other evidence, as we shall see, tends to favour the second hypothesis.

The question of prompting and confirmation has already cropped up in association with motor and perceptual skills. In a set of experiments Cook and Kendler (1956), Cook (1958) and Cook and Spitzer (1960) used a classical paired-associate task similar to a linear multiple-choice program under two conditions. In the first, the prompting condition, the stimulus term and then the response term are shown before *S* makes his response. In the second, the confirmation procedure, the subject is required to respond immediately after the stimulus and is then shown the correct response term. In these experiments the prompting technique proved to be superior. The logical conclusion from these and the previously described multiple-choice experiments would seem to be that the most effective way of learning is to be told the correct answer. Finding the correct answer only after first having got it wrong may well be only second best. Such a simple-minded approach would suggest that K R *per se* is irrelevant to the main issue of learning.

We now come to Skinner who holds explicitly that K R is reinforcing. His original design for a teaching machine was based on the premise that normal teaching methods did not provide sufficient reinforcements. By analogy with operant conditioning in animals, teaching consists of shaping behaviour by (a) providing a situation in which progressively better approximations to the desired performance are possible, and (b) correct behaviour is immediately reinforced. These conditions are provided by the short step linear program, where the verbal form of the frame is usually adequate to prompt a correct response. The correct response is then immediately confirmed. By careful sequencing a repertoire of responses is then built up. Skinner (1954, 1958) has always insisted that it is the confirmation of the correct response which is crucial to learning. It is therefore not surprising that the challenge has been taken up by a series of experimenters who have attempted various manipulations of the confirmation. Evans (1960) gave immediate and delayed K R in a symbolic logic program and found no difference. Meyer (1960) on the other hand found that in a linear spelling program immediate self-scoring gave better results than not having the correct answer and leaving the scoring to the teacher. Since the error rate was fairly high (about 14 per cent) and many students made many more errors, one suspects that in the Pressey type program, confirmation was in fact giving students new information. Almost every other study has failed to obtain significant differences between reinforced and unreinforced practice with linear programs having a low error rate (Feldhusen and Birt, 1962; Holland, 1966; Hough and Revsin, 1963; McDonald and Allen, 1962; Moore and Smith, 1961, 1964; Culclasure, 1964; Ripple, 1963; Evans, 1964; Oppenheim, 1964; Becker, 1964; Dannenberg, 1965; Jacobs and Kulkarni, 1966).

The finding 'no significant difference' has been very common in the field of programmed learning and one must be careful in interpreting these results. Being unable to demonstrate a difference does not prove that there are no differences to be found given a sensitive measure. Many results in programmed learning are based on rather short passages of program where, for example, novelty effect could mask other effects. The test instruments used for measuring learning effects are also important. In most cases immediate retention of the material in the program is tested; less often delayed retention and transfer are measured, yet these could be more sensitive indicators of the depth and persistence of learning. Despite these cautions in interpreting experimental findings one cannot help being struck by the consistency over a number of studies and by the difference between results obtained with Pressey-type programs, where responses are not heavily prompted and error rate is generally fairly high, and Skinner type programs, where responses *are* heavily prompted and error rate is usually low. The evidence here and in the prompting studies is consistent with the view that KR is valuable only when the supporting material does not by itself convey all the information.

Reinforcement in linear programs has been varied in ways other than simply presence versus absence of the confirmation frame. Evans (1960) found no deleterious effects of short delay in confirmation in a linear program or

symbolic logic. Ottina (1964) used a multiple-choice program with either high or low cue content and either
immediate confirmation or a ten-second delay. The only
significant difference to emerge was that subjects working
with high cue content and no delay worked faster. In a
paced presentation, Parkinson (1964) added nine seconds
to the time the stimulus frame was presented for one
group and nine seconds to the time the confirmation frame
was presented for another group. When compared with
each other and controls, no significant learning difference
emerged but there was an interaction with ability, lower
ability subjects doing better with more time to read the
confirmation frame. Boersma (1965) set out to control
intertrial intervals and confirmation delay interval which
are often experimentally confounded. In a factorial design
using either 0 or 8 seconds delay in confirmation and
either 0 or 8 seconds delay in the post-confirmation interval, that is before the next frame, no significant difference
emerged. It would appear then, that short delays are not
critical and expensive machinery to give immediate K R is
unnecessary. However, that is not to say that longer delays
running into days are not to be avoided as suggested by
Meyer's (1960) results.

On the superficial extension of the analogy between
human programmed learning and animal operant conditioning, partial reinforcement seems an interesting variable. Although reinforcing less than 100 per cent of
responses may give slower learning, certain partial schedules can lead to slower extinction, hence the method
might be superior when retention is the dependent
variable. The analogy is, however, only superficial as
pointed out by Amsel (1960). In the human case the subject matter progresses, new response elements being added
by each frame. In the animal case it is usually a matter of
changing the rate at which a single response is emitted.
Nevertheless there have been several studies of partial
reinforcement in the form of omitting confirmation on a
given proportion of frames. Evans (1964) varied, amongst

other things, the percentage reinforcement, either 100
per cent or 50 per cent and found no differences on a criterion test attributable to this variable. Oppenheim (1964)
compared 100 per cent, intermittent and no confirmation
at all and found no significant difference. Driskill (1964)
comparing 100 per cent and 40 per cent reinforcement on
both immediate post-test and a seven-day retention test
again found no differences. Krumboltz and Kiesler (1965)
using no less than six degrees of reinforcement by modify-
ing both the number of questions asked and the number
of confirmations given, did find some advantages to a high
level of reinforcement. The more reinforcement the fewer
errors were made and the more subjects liked the task.
However, long-term retention measured two months later
showed no difference attributable to reinforcement conditions. It appears, therefore, that Amsel's view that intermittent confirmation is not analogous to partial reinforcement is correct. Indeed it is not unfair to suggest that on
the basis of a considerable amount of evidence no simple
analogy between confirmation and operant reinforcement
stands up, a conclusion foreshadowed by Hilgard (1963).
'It has turned out that Skinner's confidence, whilst important in promoting programmed learning, has not been
fully sustained ... this follows in part because the analogies
he used are just that, and do not necessarily represent
identities in the processes involved in Skinner boxes and
programmed learning' (p. 237).

5 Incentives

The question of motivation has provided psychology with some of its most persistent problems. Theorists have tended to gravitate to one of two poles. Cognitive theorists who emphasize the intellectual, rational or information processing aspects of behaviour run the risk of leaving the organism 'rapt in thought' with no apparent motive to do anything. On the other hand, those who emphasize drives, motives and need tend to paint a picture of the organism at the mercy of the simpler and stronger biological urges, stumbling irrationally from one deprivation state to another without pausing to think. Both these pictures have elements of truth and falsity. Whichever point of view his initial prejudices favour, the student of behaviour has a problem – either the problem of showing how simple responses governed by basic needs develop into complex behaviour or the problem of providing the essential motive power to a sophisticated machine. Our task in this chapter is to look at some of the investigations of the motivational functions of KR.

At least two kinds of motivational functions have been attributed to KR – an *incentive effect* and a *reinforcing effect*. The so-called incentive effect refers to the empirical property of KR in enhancing some measure of performance such as speed, accuracy or effort. The reinforcing effect refers to the role of KR in producing more or less permanent behaviour changes, the ability to remember a paired-associate item or the correct turn at a choice point. In both cases the dependent variable is a change in behaviour, and one way of distinguishing between incentive and reinforcing effects depends on what kind of change of behaviour is being considered. Not all changes in behaviour are called learning; for example, changes brought about by

the administration of drugs. Some of these change
brought about by incentives are remarkably similar
these; they are fairly dramatic and transitory. By learnin
we generally mean more permanent changes and so
distinction between incentive and reinforcement migh
depend on where one draws the line regarding the per
manence of the behaviour changes. Some theorists prefe
not to make such a distinction. For instance, either a rat o
a human pulling a lever for a reward will tend to increas
the rate of lever pulling when the rewards are frequent an
the rate of pulling will fall off when the reward no longe
comes. Since this transitory process is generally terme
learning and extinction, we can see that the distinction be
tween incentive and reinforcement is a difficult one t
make in terms of current usage. Nevertheless, one migh
make a distinction in terms of the nature of the dependen
variable. Where measures of speed or effort and, in som
cases, accuracy are concerned, we normally will refer to th
incentive effect. Where the dependent variable concern
choice between responses or the accuracy of responses, w
refer to the reinforcement effect. Where the behaviou
changes do not long outlast the provision of KR, we refe
to incentives, and where the changes appear to be of a mor
permanent character, we refer to reinforcement.

Before we leave the distinction between incentive an
reinforcement as settled (even if arbitrarily so) there ar
several more points to make. The essential nature of the
incentive is that the physical reward is given *after* the
required change in behaviour. The worker changes from a
state of sloth to one of feverish activity *before* he gets hi
bonus and then generally he will stop. There is obviously
a potential source of confusion here. If we call the reward
itself the incentive then clearly it is rather more likely to
decrease effort than to increase it. In the language of com
monsense we would say that it is the 'promise' of the re
ward which produced the effect, not the reward itself. I
then becomes necessary to invest the promise of the reward
with properties acquired from previous rewards. In the

individual case or trial we are considering, the actual reward is only effective for the next occasion a promise is
made; it has nothing to do at all with an hypothetical
one-trial experiment. Normally we do not make too much
of this problem because we run mainly multiple-trial experiments in which there is a previous history of tangible
rewards received. Nevertheless, it forces us to turn our
attention away from the relationship between the rewarded
behaviour and the reward and to look instead at the relation between the reward and the next occurrence of the
stimulus situation in which the rewarded behaviour is one
of the options.

This problem was appreciated by Thorndike, whose
critics raised the question of how the reward could act
backwards in time. Thorndike's answer, and ours, is that
the relevant process is not backward-acting but concerns
the effect of some previous reward on future behaviour.
The classical description of an incentive experiment with
the reward arriving after the rewarded effort gives the
superficial impression that we are talking about a process
working the other way. We must, however, distinguish
between situations in which the change in performance
occurs before any actual reward is applied and those in
which the change occurs only after a reward has been applied, if only for the reason that in the first case the incentive effect cannot be attributed to the specific reward given
but only to some previously given reward. If behaviour
changes after the subject has been given a piece of chocolate, we might attribute the change to the chocolate. If the
change occurs before the chocolate is given, then it must
be attributed to something else (the promise of chocolate
if you like). It is important to make this distinction when
establishing the incentive value of different stimuli.

Thus it emerges that an incentive stimulus is very often
not in itself a substantive reward. This leads to the further
point that even in experiments where rewards like food
and water are given, these are insufficient to satisfy physiological needs. In a typical operant conditioning experi-

ment the hungry animal is fed only small quantities of food at a time. If he were allowed to eat his fill, responses would no longer be forthcoming. In the parallel human experiments, subjects are often given small quantities of money for small increments in a score. Given the full amount they must earn in the experiment, they would no longer have an incentive to work. This raises another distinction between incentive effects and reinforcing effects which again is a source of some semantic confusion. It is commonly asserted that incentives *increase* drive. This is empirically the case if by increasing drive we mean the subject works harder. On the other hand most reinforcement theories of learning assert that reinforcement *reduces* drive. Since both incentives and reinforcers are normally what we would, in plain language, call rewards this conclusion seems paradoxical. Certainly rewards and reinforcers are such things as food when hungry, and if one envisages drive as a degree of deprivation, then even a small reward will to some extent reduce the total amount or degree of deprivation. If, on the other hand, we define drive differently, that is to say, in terms of the effort the subject will make to get the reward, then the statement that a small quantity of the desired reward will increase drive is generally true. The paradox then depends on different formal definitions of drive, either as a degree of deprivation or as an amount of goal-oriented striving. Degree of deprivation is the measure mainly used in animal experimentation and is readily measured in terms of, for example, the ratio of hunger to *ad lib* feeding, body weight or simply hours of deprivation. Effort has also been used as a measure of drive by animal experimenters, but it is especially valuable for human experimentation where deprivation procedures are seldom used and, in any case, give only the crudest measure. The deprivation measure, however, makes it virtually impossible to define drive reduction quantitatively. That drive has been reduced is, in fact, a pure inference unless one takes a measure of level of performance. From this point of view it could be argued that in an operant conditioning experiment the extinction curve gives better evidence of drive reduction than the learning curve.

To summarize the foregoing points, it would be misleading simply to equate incentives with physical rewards. An incentive is in some sense the promise which produces changes in behaviour before any reward is given. Furthermore physical rewards act as incentives only if they are given in quantities too small in themselves to be satisfying or fully drive reducing. For the remainder of this chapter we shall concentrate on incentives and the question of reinforcement will be taken up in chapter 6.

These are just some of the semantic problems which surround the topic of motivation and its role in learning and performance. Despite some of the obvious difficulties we will now turn to the data. In view of our everyday knowledge, or at least opinions, that incentives increase levels of performance, experimentation would seem superfluous. But beyond the scientific urge to check up on common sense lies the need to know more about the functioning of incentives. What kinds of stimuli have incentive value, what changes can they bring about and how big and how durable are these changes? Overall hangs the problem of elucidating the mechanism that makes behaviour possible.

Financial Incentives

The most obvious human incentive is, of course, money paid for real work. Field studies in industry, e.g. Wyatt (1934), have generally confirmed our suspicions, although the operation of incentive schemes in industry is often based on such complex relationships between what is actually done and pay-off that they run into difficulties. Taking an academic point of view, Opsahl and Dunnette (1966) are not too satisfied with the rigour of field studies on incentives. They also point out that whilst people in general behave *as if* they were working for money, the response to questionnaires suggests cash is far from being the most important pay-off for work.

Taking the study of financial rewards into the laboratory, as has been done by a number of experimenters, may permit more rigorous control but introduces other problems. To middle-class students small cash payments for a few hours spent voluntarily in the laboratory may have a totally different significance from the bonuses paid to a stevedore with ten children and a lot of hire-purchase commitments. As with most other commodities, the value of money is almost certainly not a linear function of quantity, and the shape of the function is probably related in some way to the current state of supply. Nevertheless quantities of money have been used, for example, by Thorndike and Lorge (1935), who used French money to improve accuracy in a throwing task. Among recent studies, Tombaugh and Marx (1963) varied the amount of money from 1 cent up to 5 cents and from 5 cents down to 1 cent in increasing and decreasing schedules. The increasing amount of money was related to extinction on an operant task, the increasing schedule giving greater resistance to extinction. Swets and Sewell (1963) (see chapter 3) found no additional value from financial incentives in training and auditory and detection tasks. Toppen (1965a, b and c, 1966) systematically varied the amounts of money which could be earned by subjects by pulling a lever $\frac{5}{8}$ inches against 25 lb pressure. Using variable ratio schedules, the apparatus was designed to pay off for one in 100, one in 500 or one in 2500 responses, and would pay 1 cent, 5 cents or 25 cents. In this situation the value or utility of any work done will be the product of the amount paid and the frequency of pay-offs. The result showed that the cost of effort, i.e. the number of pulls, was more or less related to pay-off, although the data were somewhat variable. In a further experiment, Toppen (1965b) using a single ratio of 1/1000 progressively increased or decreased the amount of money paid off. Whilst the decreasing values led to lower rates in performance, the increasing values did not always achieve higher output. It is difficult to say whether this result is due to increasing physical fatigue or whether the non-linearity of the value of money is being demonstrated. In a third study, Toppen (1965c) demonstrated, as had Wyatt *et al.* (1934), that piece rate leads to greater effort than flat time payment. One group of subjects was given $1,50 at the beginning of the session and told they could pull the lever if they felt like it. The second group was paid 10 cents for each 1000 pulls. A result in favour of piece rate is hardly surprising but, in view of some other results on verbal (non-financial) incentives, proves nothing about the efficiency of money *per se* as an incentive. As we shall see, the nature of the instructions given the subjects is vital. In his fourth study, Toppen (1966) had subjects work for five successive one-hour sessions maintaining the pay-off constant for one group and gradually reducing it for another group. The second group's performance tailed off and absenteeism grew as the rewards shrank.

These studies of financial incentives leave a number of questions to be answered. The generalization that people will work harder for more money is only partially true, and greater reliability can be placed on the statement that they work less hard as the reward is reduced. The relative failure of increasing amounts of money to stimulate proportionately increased effort could indicate either that physiological limits are being approached or that the value of money does not increase linearly with absolute quantity.

Symbolic Incentives

In much of the work on incentives in the laboratory, no material reward is given but subjects are given knowledge of results. Most of these studies involve tasks of a repetitive, monotonous or fatiguing kind, and, although some learning might occur, they are generally rather simple tasks and the relevant dependent variables are to do more with the maintenance of performance levels than with the initial acquisition of skills. Typical early studies were by Arps (1917) and Crawley (1926). Arps showed that performance on an ergograph was improved by giving K R and that work without K R was dull and subjects were said to be poorly motivated. Crawley had four subjects lifting weights to the beat of a metronome almost to the point of exhaustion. On being able to watch a kymographic record of their efforts they recovered completely and even exceeded the limits of performance reached on 'non-incentive' trials. After removal of K R, however, performance dropped below the original level.

Monitoring tasks, whilst not physically exhausting show performance decrements – namely, a fall in the detection rate over time – and the effects of simply giving subjects information about their performance has been extensively studied. Mackworth (1950) used a device known as the clock test, a circular dial round which a pointer moved in discrete steps once every second, the dial being divided into 100 such steps. Very occasionally the pointer moved through two steps at once, and this was the signal the subjects were required to detect. Normally subjects were quite isolated during a two-hour watch and failures to detect normally increased from about 15 per cent to about 30 per cent of signals presented over that period. In one experiment (clock test 5) subjects were told that they would get instructions from time to time via a telephone. In fact they all got a message after about one hour telling them to do better. This had a dramatic but temporary effect on performance (Figure 8). In another experiment (clock test 7), the experimenter reported verbally to the subject on any response or failure to respond. With knowledge of results the progressive decrement over the two-hour watch was virtually abolished but there was still a tendency to increase rather than reduce errors. Some subjects did two runs, one with and one without knowledge of results. The beneficial effect of giving K R for the first session appeared to extend over into the second no-K R session, whilst the introduction of K R following no-KR brought about the expected improvement. This suggests a certain diffuseness in the effects of KR which one might expect if the information were being used to control the subject's overall strategy rather than being used more specifically as an aid to individual detections. The Mackworth result, is however, none too clear, since the group getting KR first were, for unknown reasons, rather poor performers initially. This point was followed up in further experiments in auditory detection. The task

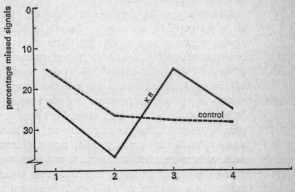

Figure 8   Effects of KR *at beginning of period 3 (Mackworth, 1950)*

here was a simulated Asdic (sonar) 'ping' followed by re-verberations. Occasionally a fainter ping could be heard in the reverberations about one and a half seconds later. In this experiment (main listening test 2), subjects performed a two-hour watch twice, once with and once without KR as for clock test 7. Without KR detections fell off but with KR detections increased slightly over the two hours. This experiment confirmed that the effects of KR extended to a second watch given a day later.

In an exhaustive study, Hauty and Payne (1955) and

Payne and Hauty (1955) used a multiple tracking task. The subjects observed an array of four dials on each of which a pointer was either at a desired setting or out of tolerance. Out of tolerance settings were corrected by the movement of a control stick and subjects performed a seven-hour stint. In a complex design the effects of drugs, knowledge of results and set goals were investigated. In this case, there is fairly obvious 'intrinsic' K R from the dial displays, but by adding a warning light or a warning buzzer additional K R was furnished. Performance levels were found to be higher with the additional K R, but decrement over the duration of the task was not prevented. In a second experiment, Payne and Hauty (1955) gave various kinds of knowledge of results with the intention of differentiating informational and motivational effects of K R on the same task. In addition to the four dials, one condition provided a warning light indicating that there was a deviation, whilst in a second condition warning lights showed which dial was out of tolerance. For the incentive conditions information was given to subjects about their standing relative to a group mean, or subjects were also given returns relative to their own previous performance; thus the incentive conditions gave information about performance standards. The control for all these conditions, information as well as incentive, was the basic task, including its own intrinsic K R. Both directive and incentive K R were found to be effective in raising performance levels, but some interesting differences between the two emerged. Contrary to Mackworth's results, directional K R did not affect work decrement, whilst incentive K R increased its effect for the first hour and decreased thereafter. It could thus be said to postpone decrement rather than abolish it. Although here appear to be contradictions between these and Mackworth's results, there are too many differences between the two sets of experiments for us to be clear about their origins. Mackworth's subjects were on watch for only two hours, whilst Payne and Hauty's were on watch for seven hours and in a fundamentally different kind of design, with some subjects undergoing different treatments on different days including various drug treatments as well.

Between the physically fatiguing tasks and those requiring mainly perceptual vigilance, a range of other monotonous perceptual-motor tasks has been used. For example, Ross (1927) had subjects cancel sets of lines, Mace (1935) had subjects perform routine calculations, Gibbs and Brown (1955) had subjects copy pages from reports and encyclopedias on a copying machine, and Chapanis (1964) had subjects prepare computer tapes of random numbers. As in the ergographic tasks, the relevant performance measure is in terms of work output, rather than in detection rate, although accuracy is also a secondary measure. Among those studies in which subjects were given KR, only Chapanis (1964) failed to find an incentive effect. He compared four groups who performed this task over twenty-four days. Group 1 was given no indication of the amount of work required or the amount completed, group 2 had a counter recording their work but attention was not specially drawn to this and it was never reset. Group 3 had the counter reset to zero at the beginning of each one-hour session, and group 4 were asked to record the counter reading at fifteen, thirty and forty-five minutes but were told that this information was for accounting purposes only. Although performance of all four groups improved over the twenty-four days, there was no difference between the groups with different amounts of information. This is in marked contrast to Mace's (1935) study where subjects were given specific instructions about the targets they should attempt to achieve. In Mace's computation task, for example, all subjects received information on the number of computations per session, but received different instructions concerning their performance targets. One group was told simply to do their best, another was given a target of seventy computations per ten-minute period, and a third was given the target of exceeding the previous day's performance. Mace empha-

no you)
reedback

sizes that the purpose of the scoring system was to 'direct attention to the standard prescribed'. The numbers, it was claimed, did not possess any pronounced reward value to the subjects. The main result was that subjects who were simply told to do their best improved faster and reached a higher level in twenty days than those given an absolute performance standard, and that these were better than subjects working to the relative standards.

Not all experimenters distinguish between the K R given and instructions about targets. In many cases the provision of K R may be taken by subjects as implying a standard of performance but, as Chapanis's results showed, this is not necessarily the case. Brown (1966), in replying to Chapanis's criticisms of the Gibbs and Brown experiment, pointed out that only when a K R or a no-K R condition was given *second*, the alternative condition having been experienced previously, is there any differential effect; that is to say, K R improves performance if the task has previously been done without it. Whilst it would be dangerous to speculate on the reasons for success and failure of K R in particular cases, these results do point in the direction of something other than sheer K R *per se* as being important. Mace expressed his view on this distinction most clearly. For him the concept of an *intention* or target was an integral part of the incentive.

So, generally, whatever incentive or incentive conditions may be employed, the performance of any task is throughout controlled by some specific intention, commonly the intention to perform a determinate set of movements resulting in some industrial product conforming to certain standards. The specific intention is thus the focal point in the study of incentives (Mace, 1935, p. 2).

Since 1935 it has become distinctly unfashionable to use such mentalistic terms as 'intention'; nevertheless some concept of the aim or goal of the performer does seem to be necessary in order to deal with the effects of incentives. In human subjects at least, incentives are manipulable both through instructions and through knowledge of past performance.

As a result of a series of experiments using the computational task, an aiming task and a ball-and-slot task (in which a box containing ball bearings is manipulated so as to get as many as possible into a single slot), Mace concluded that 'the efficiency with which mental and physical operations are performed depends to some considerable degree upon the standards implicitly or explicitly, wittingly or unwittingly, adopted by the worker' (1935, p. 51).

The effect of K R as such is to provide information about the standard. The aiming experiment illustrates what is meant. Circular targets with a bullseye 1 mm in diameter and nine concentric rings 1 mm apart were fixed onto the wall at eye level. Subjects had a single shot at each of 150 targets in rapid succession. There were no rewards and subjects were simply instructed to do their best. In a second condition, however, subjects were also told of their average error on the previous ten targets. One group of subjects did thirteen sessions of no-K R followed by thirteen sessions of K R, and a second group did the reverse. The results show that the introduction of K R gives an immediate improvement to performance greater than that attained from all thirteen practice periods.

The suggestion that it is not simply knowledge *per se* but some attitude towards performance standards is demonstrated by the results of these experiments. In the computation task all groups, whether during receiving extrinsic K R or not, improved steadily during the course of the experiment. Naturally, all had at least some idea of how many calculations they were getting through. But at the same time it was the group urged simply to do their best which surpassed the other groups given actual knowledge of the number of completed calculations. Mace is undoubtedly justified in insisting on some kind of concept of intention in addition to the reward of realizing the intention.

In a recent series of studies Locke (1966a, 1966b) and

Locke and Bryan (1966a, 1966b), have attempted to clarify the notion of intention and its interaction with results. In a series of tasks in which different standards of successful performance were set, Locke (1966a) found that productivity was more or less a linear function of the performance target. These tasks consisted of giving names of objects described by a given adjective or listing uses for given objects, and both target and performance measure was simply the number of words produced. In a complex co-ordination task (Locke and Bryan, 1966a, 1966b), subjects were required to produce a pattern of display lights with a corresponding pattern produced by moving a joystick and a foot-pedal control. A comparison was made between simply letting subjects do their best and giving them a target corresponding to their previous test score plus fifteen points increment. The results showed that the setting of a specified standard led to both a faster rate of improvement and an overall higher standard. In this experiment, as in Mace's aiming task, intrinsic K R was available to the subject by virtue of the nature of the apparatus.

In a repeat of Mace's computation experiment, Locke and Bryan (1966b) produced further evidence that the nature of the goal or intention rather than K R affects performance. Three groups of subjects were asked to perform complex computations for six successive ten-minute periods. Two groups received knowledge of the number of correct computations in each period and marked these on their work sheets, but one of these groups was given the instruction to get a score of fifteen more than their previous best on each trial. A third group was given minimal K R by listening to the correct answers being read out by experimenter, but they were not required to check their score or to better their performance. All groups were questioned after the experiment about the goals they set themselves. The three conditions did not differentially affect output, but subjective goals did. All subjects were classified on the basis of their replies into those who tried to beat the standard, those simply aiming to better their score, those only aiming to do their best, and the remainder who admitted poor motivation. These categories of responses were fairly well distributed over the four treatments, so the fact that E sets a standard cannot be taken as evidence that S adopts it. The output was highest for those attempting to do their best and those simply attempting to improve performance, with poorly motivated subjects providing not much more than half the number of calculations provided by the highly motivated group. These results do justify some distinction between the effect of having a standard and simply having K R. K R can be the means by which a standard is specified and a means by which S can relate his performance to the standard, but knowledge *per se* does not necessarily have an incentive effect at all.

Conclusion

Having examined the 'motivating' or incentive function attributed to K R, we may ask if this can be differentiated from informative functions. Where does motivation fit into a feedback description of behaviour? Is motivation something which has to be added to an information processing feedback system in order to, as it were, bring it to life? The short answer is quite simply that *a fully operative feedback system does not need any additional factor.* If we return to the servo-mechanism described in chapter 1, it is not difficult to see that there is little difference in principle between this device taking corrective action to maintain a given speed and an organism taking corrective action to maintain a full stomach. Motivation could be described as feedback in action. If we look at the parts of the simple servo, the general truth of this statement becomes apparent. The electric motor is supplied by a source of power. At first sight the source of power appears to be a candidate for the role of 'motive' or 'drive'. If there is no power available the mechanism will not work, or if the power available is not enough to compensate for the load conditions the motor output will fall short of the target. There is a limit of exhaustion beyond which no carrot will persuade the donkey to move. But here we are thinking of a general pool of energy which is available to the organism (or mechanism). However, motivation implies not just the availability of energy for consumption, but the direction of the activity to some goal. Feedback itself is often said to provide motivation, but the mere existence of a feedback loop does not guarantee goal-directed activity until some value for target output has been specified and an 'error signal' can be generated which can then be fed back to control the power supply. Thus no one part of the system can properly be said to provide 'motivation' even though each part is indispensable.

These points can be illustrated from the experiments we have just reviewed. That the availability of K R without any specified performance standard or target to home onto is not 'motivating' is clearly demonstrated in Chapanis's experiment. Subjects provided with a performance counter but not given any target did not show any strong tendency to improve their performance. As Mace demonstrated, the provision of a standard by means of instructions often raises performance levels without K R. But we must not take the absence of K R too literally for all his tasks contained ample intrinsic K R. When the aim is simply to exceed a given output, detailed information is not very vital since the subject is capable of making the rough distinction between increased effort and decreased effort on the basis of intrinsic feedback. Another feature of the results was that when K R was removed performance levels did not always return to their original par. K R can include *or* imply information about the standard of performance required where this has not been given in previous instructions; once the performance standard is known, it will not normally be forgotten, so, provided some intrinsic K R is available, performance will not necessarily drop when K R is removed. The finding that fairly wide variations in the magnitude of financial rewards do not produce correspondingly large changes in performance and that purely symbolic rewards work just as well is consistent with the feedback concept of motivation. If, as is suggested, the role of feedback is to signal error information which releases corrective action, it may not matter very much if this information is signalled in pennies, dollars, pounds or 'glubs'.

In conclusion, it seems that the feedback model fits the data on incentives well enough, but the implication is that incentive effects are not basically different from 'informational' effects. If motivation is quite simply feedback in action, the T O T E unit for hammering nails or tracking a target is as much an example of motivated behaviour as a T O T E unit for quenching thirst.

6 Reinforcement

The concept of reinforcement has already been outlined in
the introductory chapter, and, as we have seen, the term
has been used in a number of senses. In its weak sense, reinforcement is a descriptive term. Anything which leads to
the selective repetition of previous behaviour or increases
the probability of a given response to a specific stimulus
situation is, in this sense, a reinforcer. Reinforcement in this
sense has no explanatory value. We cannot attribute learning to reinforcement simply because we define reinforcers
as those stimuli or events which have a reinforcing effect.

In the strong sense of the term, as classically used by
Thorndike and Hull, reinforcement is not purely descriptive, it does entail assumptions about the mechanism of
learning and this particular hypothesis, the Law of Effect,
has to do with motivation. Essentially, the hypothesis is
that learning occurs when some need or drive is reduced by
the provision of a reward. Learning is the increased in-
cidence of the rewarded behaviour, and, in human subjects at least, the reward is a secondary or conditioned
reinforcer, usually in the form of knowledge of results. The
classical instances of the supposed operation of the Law of
Effect are, of course, Thorndike's line-drawing and paired-
associate learning experiments (Thorndike, 1931, 1932,
1933a and b). These experiments and the effect hypothesis
have drawn the fire of a number of investigators and we shall
now look at some of the attempts which have been made to
establish or refute the existence of an effect mechanism.

Additional Rewards and Punishments

One line of attack is to suggest that verbal reinforcers
(such as K R) promote learning not because they are re-

warding (i.e. drive reducing) but because they provide information. There have been numerous attempts to solve the problem of distinguishing between informational and reinforcing effects – none entirely satisfactory. It could be argued that a test of this hypothesis could be made if it were possible to manipulate reward independently of the information contained in K R. One of the earliest attempts to do this was by Bunch (1928) who used Carr's stylus maze, a matrix of holes into which a stylus is inserted. In some holes an electrical contact is made. Two groups of subjects learned the maze, one group by normal trial-and-error and a second group receiving electric shocks for each blind alley entered. This arrangement provides the two groups with the same information about what is right and what is wrong, whilst introducing punishment for one group. It does not, however, rule out the possibility that correct responses are rewarding in some way, and it could be argued that punishment *per se*, in any case, is rather ineffective as a negative reinforcer. As it turned out there was more than one difference between the two groups. The punishment group learned in half the trials making overall 30 per cent less errors, but at the same time their performance was much more slow and circumspect and it was clear that the introduction of punishment was affecting the way the subjects tackled the task.

Tolman, Hall and Bretnall (1932) (see also chapter 4) improved on this experiment by running two conditions in which some subjects received a shock for the wrong response and others a shock for the correct response. Subjects getting the 'shock-for-correct' treatment learned in fewer trials than those getting 'shock-for-wrong'. A similar experiment was done by Hulin and Katz (1935) using a bell with the Tolman punchboard maze. The 'bell-for-correct' group learned in an average of 10·3 trials as against 11·9 for the 'bell-for-wrong' group and made 58·2 as opposed to 76 errors on average. The advantage in favour of the 'bell-for-correct' group is not dramatic.

Gilbert and Crafts (1935) found only small and insigni-

ficant differences between two groups learning a maze
where one group had a click after every error and another
group a shock. In a later study, Bernard and Gilbert (1941)
did find some differences between learning cul-de-sacs
which resulted in a shock and those which simply presented a barrier. A stylus maze was arranged such that
some subjects received a shock in some cul-de-sacs but not
in others. With a second group the shock and non-shock
errors were reversed to equate for possible differences in
difficulty between the arbitrarily chosen shock and non-
shock alleys. In both groups the shocked cul-de-sacs were
eliminated more quickly.

As a result of his experiments and others such as those
just described, Tolman concluded that the Law of Effect
had been refuted. Certainly on a straightforward interpretation it looks very much like it, but on closer examination, the matter is not quite so simple. The fault with the
'punishment-for-correct' situation is that learning might
be attributable solely to the rewarding effects of being
right. Tolman's experiment with shock-for-right would
seem on the face of it to eliminate the reward value of
correct response, but this is only true if one is dealing
solely with primary reinforcement. In its later version,
Thorndike's Law of Effect really referred to secondary
reinforcement. He envisaged that any one of a whole
variety of signals, which might include electric shocks,
could trigger off an 'O K reaction' and that it was the O K
reaction which provided the reinforcement. This modifica-
tion makes Thorndike's theory immune to this kind of
attack and also has the convenient consequence that almost any kind of stimulus can act as a 'reward'. The fact
that the O K reaction is only inferred and is unobservable
does, of course, weaken the theory, for it must then follow
that the direct manipulation of supposedly motivational
variables by ordinary rewards and punishments is now
irrelevant.

However, taking these experiments at their face value,
two things are demonstrated. The first is that strong

punishment can affect the general pattern of behaviour in the learning situation and this itself could have an indirect effect on learning. The second is that where situations are informationally equivalent, a strong stimulus such as a shock or bell does add a little, but perhaps not very much, to the efficiency of learning. It would be unwise to go beyond this, as Tolman did, and assert that the learning is merely due to the *emphasis* given by rewards and punishments. It would seem that basically subjects learn what there is to be learnt and emphasis of strong stimuli affects learning and performance only marginally.

Given that a reward cannot be, as it were, 'blacked out' by the superimposition of a punishing stimulus and that the information 'you are correct' can never be shown to be entirely neutral in the sense of being devoid of rewarding consequences, another way of tackling the problem is to attempt to add additional rewards to 'neutral' information. We have already seen that increasing the magnitude of monetary rewards does not produce any dramatic effects on performance levels. In the field of animal experiments, the manipulation of magnitude of primary rewards has not in general been found to lead to gross differences in learning (Pubols, 1960).

Thorndike's concept of the 'O K reaction' is convenient here, since, provided the reward reached a threshold value sufficient to trigger the O K reaction, no further increase in the magnitude of reward would be effective. Nevertheless, there have been several attempts to add 'rewarding feedback' to 'informative feedback'. Morin (1951) using a lever positioning task varied the apparent size of the target without varying the accuracy required to score a hit. For one group the target was indicated by a single light in a bank of lights and in a second group, the same target was indicated by three adjacent lights. A third group had, in addition, a bell for a hit plus a cumulative score of successes. No differences in learning were discovered. Bilodeau (1951), in a similar task with a rudder control instead of a joystick, used social competition as an added incentive to the intrinsic K R. Subjects were tested on speed and accuracy of rudder positioning either alone or in pairs and for part or whole of the test. Again no differences emerged between the groups. Travis (1938) added both monetary rewards and shock to the intrinsic K R in a tracking task. One group was given a reward after alternate trials and another a shock on alternate trials. In both cases the rewards and punishments were unrelated to actual responses. Performance turned out to be better on both rewarded and punished trials than on 'neutral' trials, with the advantage slightly in favour of punishment. Bahrick, Fitts and Rankin (1952) reported that a graded monetary reward resulted in increased selectivity of perception such that subjects did much better on parts of the task for which they thought they were being rewarded and did rather worse on other parts of the task. All in all, these studies seem to have demonstrated little more than that the addition of rewards as well as the addition of punishments can affect the subjects' style of performance and thus indirectly affect the efficiency of learning, but there is no direct evidence that increasing the magnitude of reward increased the strength of the reinforcement. We may conclude that this kind of attempt to test the Law of Effect is rather fruitless and, moreover, that in one form the law is quite immune to this kind of test.

Effects of Instructions to Learn

As we have seen, stimuli one would normally classify as rewards and punishments (e.g. money and electric shock) do not have the simple effects which would appear to be required for a straighforward Law of Effect, but the damage this does to the standing of the law can be repaired by the concept of the 'O K reaction' which can be triggered by any kind of stimulus, even a noxious one. The simple statement 'that's right' or some symbolic equivalent should then trigger the O K reaction and learning should occur. Another attack on the Law of Effect is the demonstration that there are certain circumstances in which the O K reaction is not triggered off, that is to say, the symbolic reward 'O K' or 'that's right' does not result in learning. Mention has already been made of experiments of this kind by Wallach and Henle (1941, 1942) and by Nuttin (1953).

Wallach and Henle used a typical Thorndikian learning task consisting of a very long list of stimulus items each requiring the subject to produce a response which was immediately followed by the statement 'right' or 'wrong'. Stimulus items were repeated such that any increase in the frequency of 'right' responses could be noted. The one major difference between this and many of the experiments reported by Thorndike was that subjects were informed that they were participating in an E S P experiment rather than a learning task. Under these instructions, no permanent connexion between a given S and any specific R was implied. Subjects had no reason to believe (and in fact were discouraged from believing) that a response which was correct to a given stimulus on one occasion would be correct on the next occasion. Under these conditions, the frequency of 'rewarded' responses did not increase in the slightest.

Nuttin has described a series of experiments in which the subject's attitude to the learning task is shown to be considerably more important than the simple occurrence of rewards. Like Wallach and Henle he adapted some of Thorndike's tasks to this purpose. Using an apparatus known as the Michotte Kinesiometer, in which the blindfold subject places his arm in a trough and moves it through an arc pivoted at the elbow, Nuttin produced the following variation on the line-drawing experiment. Subjects were required to make pairs of movements of varying lengths. In the first of each pair, S moved his arm against a mechanical stop. The arm was then returned to the zero position, the stop removed and S was required to repeat as exactly as possible, the movement he had just made. Second responses within 2° of the original were rewarded by the statement 'right'. Unlike the Wallach and Henle experiments, the subjects were given instructions intended to induce an intention to learn, but only with reference to any given pair of movements. The experiment consisted of making fifty such pairs of movements. The standard was always an arc of 105°, but one group of subjects was told that the movement required would be the same for each pair and another group was told that they would be different; that is to say, for one group of subjects pairs of trials were related whilst in the second group they were unrelated. At the end of training the first group had a constant error bias of 24°, whilst the second group had a constant error bias of 47°; in fact this group had hardly improved at all in achieving the actual standard of 105°.

Nuttin distinguishes between these two types of instructions by referring to those tasks in which the subject believes he is continuing to learn the same thing as 'open tasks' and those in which the subject believes he has to achieve a new goal on each trial as 'closed tasks'.

> *En résumé, la tâche ouverte met le sujet dans une situation telle que le résultat obtenu pour chacune des réponses données possède une double aspect: un aspect 'sanction', réussite ou échec, qui concerne la réponse donnée et un aspect 'information' qui se rapporte à la tâche qui reste à accomplir. ... Il est bien clair que seul le premier de ces deux aspects du résultat construire la 'recompense' ou le reduction du besoin* (Nuttin, 1953, p. 312).

To summarize, the open task puts the subject in a position such that the result obtained for each of the responses given has a double aspect: there is the aspect of 'sanction', success or failure concerning the given response and an 'informative' aspect which relates to the part of the task which is still to be completed. ... It is clear that only the first of these two aspects of the result constitutes reward or need reduction.

Of closed tasks he says

> *Une fois la réponse donnée, la tâche concernant chaque item de la série est achevée; il ne s'attend pas à devoir refaire la serie; en un mot c'est une 'tâche fermée'. Ici, le résultat*

n'est rien d'autre que le terme final *qui suit l'action de répondre. Le bon résultat ne se situe pas ici dans une perspective de l'avenir ou de tâche à achever; il n'est rien d'autre que la 'reduction du besoin de bien répondre' ou une 'recompense' dans le sens Thorndikian du term* (Nuttin, 1953, p. 313).

Once the response is given the task concerning each item of the series is achieved; there is no requirement to repeat the series; it is a closed task. Here the result is nothing more than the final term which follows the action of responding. A good result has no implications for the future or for a task still to be achieved; it is nothing more than the 'reduction of the need to make a good response' or a 'reward' in the Thorndikian sense of the term.

Certainly the pseudo E S P experiments of Wallach and Henle would be a closed task in Nuttin's sense and all the many experiments reported by Thorndike (1931, 1932, 1933) are open tasks.

At this point we might recall some earlier remarks about rewards and incentives. It is a characteristic of successful reinforcers that they do not reduce need very much. A very hungry animal is given very small quantities of food, the worker receives payment, or an indication of future payments in small gobbets related to the work he does. If full payment were made for the first correct response and the drive drastically reduced, animals would most likely not continue to work at the task. Here is at least one element of Nuttin's open-versus-closed task dichotomy. The basically unsatisfying nature of individual reinforcers is what keeps the tasks *open*, and leaves the subject with still more to accomplish before the final success and the ultimate reduction of need.

Temporal Contiguity

Whether the supposed reinforcer is believed to be a genuinely drive-reducing reward or simply a stimulus which triggers an O K reaction, the Law of Effect requires that reinforcement should be close in time to the behaviour

which is to be reinforced. Close temporal contiguity is required if the supposedly automatic nature of reinforcers is
to be preserved. Should there be an extended time interval
between the response and the reinforcer, any reinforcing
effect might have to be attributed to some mediating process and the Law of Effect would loose a good deal of its
force as an irresistable, automatic and essentially simple
biological process. In other words, if it is to be asserted
that it is only or primarily the reinforcement which preserves the s - r connexions, we have difficulty in explaining
how the connexion is preserved up to the arrival of the
reinforcer. We can, perhaps, allow a little time for the
trace to fade, but if we allow an unreinforced trace to per-
sist too long before disappearing we are allowing a
mechanism for preserving information which is independent of reinforcement as such. Where one draws the
line is entirely arbitrary but obviously the simple Law of
Effect will be more acceptable the shorter the interval required for successful learning. Two fields of research are
relevant to this question, the establishment of the *temporal gradient of reinforcement* and the *spread of effect*
(sometimes called the Thorndike effect). In the former we
are concerned with the efficiency of learning as a function
of the time elapsed between response and K R (or reinforcement); in the second we are concerned with the accidental
reinforcement of wrong responses which occur in close
temporal contiguity with correct reinforcement responses.

Except in rare cases of single trial experiments, delay is
not the simple variable it appears to be at first sight. In
multi-trial experiments it is just as true to say that K R
comes *before* responses except, of course, for the very first
one, as it is to say that it comes at an interval *after* the
response. To be precise, K R comes *between* responses so
that there are really three relevant time intervals, any two
of which determine the task. The interval relevant to the
reinforcing effect is that between the response and K R, but
in addition to this there is an interval between K R and the
next response which, if fixed inter-trials intervals are used,

gets smaller as the response–K R intervals gets larger. As Bilodeau (1966) points out, experiments have commonly confounded the effects of these intervals. Great care has to be taken to demonstrate any independent effects of delay, post-K R delay and inter-trial interval (massing and spacing). Another difficult question is the nature of the delay. Whilst it is possible for the experimenter to do nothing which affects the subject in the interval between the response and K R, there is no way of controlling what goes on in the subject's head in that interval. If the interval is at all long, the subject will undoubtedly initiate some other activity. In other words, sheer empty delay as such is a myth. Effects cannot be attributed purely to the lapse of time as such but only to whatever processes are going on during the interval. Another way of looking at the problem is to delay K R by a given number of trials. This can be done by giving individual K R trial by trial *n* trials late, or by giving the subject a summary of his performance over a given number of trials after the completion of that block of trials.

Lorge and Thorndike (1935) carried out an experiment varying both empty interval delay between response and K R and delay by trials. Subjects threw balls over the shoulder at an unseen target. Simple delays up to six seconds produced no appreciable effect on learning, but subjects failed to improve if the K R was given only one trial in arrears. Alexander (1951) repeated the empty delay part of the experiment with dart throwing and found no effect of increasing delay, although the subjects did find it increasingly difficult to make an accurate estimate of their own error with increasing delay.

Greenspoon and Foreman (1956) have reported the only positive results of delay using the line drawing task with 0, 10, 20 and 30 seconds delay. But attempts to repeat this finding by McGuigan (1959), Bilodeau and Ryan (1960), Denney, Allard, Hall and Rokeach (1960) and Becker, Mussina and Persons (1963) have all failed to confirm an effect of delay when inter-response intervals and post-K R delay are taken into account. Using a variety of positioning tasks, Bilodeau and Bilodeau (1958b) in an exhaustive study of all three temporal factors were unable to find effects due to K R delays, the shortest of which was twenty seconds and the longest seven days. In verbal tasks, much the same conclusion seems justified. Saltzman (1951) presented a series of digit pairs and subjects were told after 0, 6, 12 or 18 seconds which of the pairs was 'right'. The task was, in effect, a binary maze and increasing delay had no effect on learning the maze. However, when, in a second experiment, subjects had to reproduce the actual digits, delays were effective in reducing learning efficiency. Bourne and Bunderson (1963) found that the longer interval between K R and the next response tended to be beneficial.

Thorndike was not too unhappy about his negative finding regarding the delay of reinforcement. He was saved by the useful (Gestalt-like) principle of 'belongingness' which asserts that reinforcement is much more effective with stimulus and response items that 'belong' together. With an empty interval between response and reinforcement there is nothing to disturb this belongingness, but the insertion of even one further trial interferes with this relationship. Empty delay, if it can be achieved, is therefore not very critical to the Law of Effect.

The Spread of Effect

Far more important in Thorndike's view was the phenomenon of the *spread of effect*. This also is an essentially temporal phenomenon in which a wrong response adjacent to a rewarded response tends to be repeated even though it has been explicitly 'punished'. Thorndike saw his discovery of the spread of effect as 'an independent experimental proof of the strengthening influence of a satisfying state of affairs upon the connexion of which it is an aftereffect' (Thorndike, 1933a). Thorndike's classic result is shown in Figure 9. These results were obtained in typical paired-associate type tasks. Normally a very long list of stimulus items is presented and *S* is required to guess the response term and is then told 'right' or 'wrong'. The response term may be another word but is often a number. The phenomenon has only been found (indeed it has only

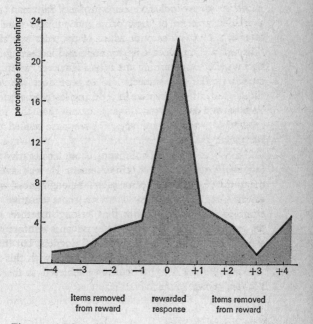

Figure 9   Thorndike's data on the spread of effect (from Thorndike, 1933a)

been sought) in these rather special conditions. A number of possible artifacts can give rise to gradients such as those found by Thorndike and others. Thorndike counted both forwards and backwards from the repeated correct response when looking for examples of repeated non-rewarded responses. This means that repeated wrong responses counted towards both fore- and after-gradients. For Thorndike's theory the gradient should be symmetri-

cal on either side of the rewarded response, but an alternative hypothesis suggests that only after-gradients exist. We
shall come to this in a moment, but in the meantime it is to
be noted that Thorndike's method of scoring was such as
to automatically produce fore-gradients. For example,
suppose a series of five responses is made. All the responses
are then repeated, only responses 1 and 5 having been rewarded. The wrong response 2 would contribute to the
after-gradient associated with response 1 and also the fore-
gradient of response 5. Similarly response 4 would contribute to the fore-gradient of response 5 as well as the
after-gradient of response 1. Responses equidistant between two rewarded responses were not counted at all, so
response 3 contributes nothing and there would be an
apparent dip between the fore- and after-gradients. This
'typical' picture of two symmetrical gradients results
simply from repeating the five responses.

Another problem is that as repetition produces more
correct responses the distance between them therefore
tends to decrease. It could be the case that stereotyped
wrong responses would therefore tend to appear nearer
and nearer to reinforced correct responses. This problem
can be avoided by keeping the number of repetitions
lower than those used by Thorndike.

Yet another problem is the choice of the appropriate
baseline for scoring repetitions. In most of Thorndike's
experiments, both correct and incorrect responses tended
to be repeated, wrong responses being repeated more than
could be expected by chance. Thorndike used as his baseline the frequency with which wrong responses occurring
more than five items from any correct response were repeated. Tilton (1945), critical of this technique, used an
empirically determined baseline by having control subjects do a guessing experiment without any K R and found
a repetition rate of 35 per cent rather than the chance level
of 25 per cent for a four-alternative multiple-choice response set. When repetitions following K R are judged by
this empirical baseline all the 'punished' responses are

found to be weakened in contrast to Thorndike's finding that even punished responses are strengthened. If a gradient does exist, some alternate hypothesis to spread of rewarding effects seems necessary since it is odd to talk of responses which have actually become weaker as being reinforced.

The most plausible alternative was suggested by Tolman and it has come to be known as the guessing sequence hypothesis. Under the conditions in which spread of effect is found, subjects are given a very difficult task in terms of the sheer amount of material and of the low probability of correct responses. The only way they can tackle it is by guessing. There is considerable evidence to show that sequences of guesses are not random but that they tend to be redundant. In a non-redundant, i.e. perfectly random, series of items, the *a priori* probability of each item is $1/n$ where n is the number of different items. Redundancy in a sequence means that guesses are not independent and that, given one item, the probability that it will be fellowed by another given item can be greater than or less than, rather than equal to $1/n$. To take a very simple two-alternative case of left and right choices, given that the first item guessed or chosen is L, the probability that the next item will be R tends to be greater than 0·5. Subjects in guessing tasks tend to produce non-redundant sequences. The reader is referred to Attneave (1959) for a clear exposition of redundancy and an experimental example of the non-randomness of guessing sequences.

The way in which this feature of guessing behaviour can produce an after-gradient such as is attributed to the spread of effect is neatly illustrated by an experiment by Sheffield (1949). Subjects were asked to produce four long lists of random numbers. These four lists were then treated as if they were the responses to paired-associate items and were set down in four columns. Reading across any row there will be occasions when the same number comes up in the same row in two adjacent columns. Now treating such repeated pairs as if the first had been a reinforced response and the second a repeat of the correct response, Sheffield counted up the frequency with which a repeated pair occurs in the next row down and in the third, fourth and fifth rows down.

His results are shown in the following table:

Position after chance repetition	Per cent of repetition
1	13·3
2	11·4
3	11·2
4	10·6
5	10·2

The result demonstrates a typical after-gradient and is due solely to the fact that subjects are unable to generate statistically random sequences. In the spread of effect experiment, repetition rates are higher than this and proponents of reinforcement have raised this as an objection to Sheffield's results. We must remember, however, that Sheffield's subjects were *trying* to produce random sequences whereas subjects with a set to learn are *trying to repeat a sequence* which they believed existed, and the redundancy would tend to be greater. Bearing in mind the effects of subtle differences in instructions illustrated by the Wallach and Henle experiments it cannot be argued, as Postman (1964) does, that Sheffield's experiment does not account for the whole effect and therefore does not rule out some spread of reinforcement.

An ingenious attempt by Marx and Goodson (1956) to eliminate the effects of guessing sequences deserves mention. A large group of schoolchildren were given a multiple-choice paired-associate task. Opposite each item in a list of twenty-seven words was a row of twelve holes into one of which *S* was told to press a stylus, rather like a twelve-alternative version of the Pressey multiple-choice system. For a 'correct' response the stylus goes right through the hole and for 'wrong' responses the stylus penetrates only a short distance. The experimenter arranged that only one, two or three responses would in fact be correct on the first trial and repetitions of 'correct' and 'incorrect' responses on the second trial were recorded. The apparatus permitted a measure of degree of repetition in terms of the number of holes by which the second response was displaced from the first, in a score of 0 to 11. It was argued that a control group had no success on trial 1, but their responses at the item rewarded in the experimental group were treated as if correct and repetitions of these and subsequent responses were recorded. Both experimental and control groups were divided into those who did and those who did not repeat the response made on the key items, thus permitting a measure of repetition following either a rewarded or a non-rewarded response. A significant after-gradient was found for 'repeaters' who had been rewarded but not for those who had not been rewarded, thus appearing to confirm that spread of effect follows a reward independently of any guessing sequences. However, both the experiment and the data are complex and the authors admit that the results are not fully consistent with either the guessing sequence hypothesis or the spread of effect. Significant gradients were found following non-repeated key responses in the experimental group and the control after-gradient was significant. A slightly worrying feature of the design was that subjects were classified as repeaters and non-repeaters on the basis of a *single* response (out of twenty-seven). We do not know whether this one response was really typical of their performance. In general one might expect subjects who had three rewards on trial 1 to tend to repeat slightly more than those who had no rewards at all. An increased tendency to repeat *all responses* in the rewarded group might be sufficient to account for the gradient on the guessing sequence hypothesis. Marx and Goodson's results represent extremely equivocal evidence in favour of a genuine reward-produced spread of effect. With so many possible artifacts and bearing in mind the known properties of guessing in this type of situation, the existence of a genuine spread of effect is very much in doubt.

Conclusion

At first sight the hypothesis that KR is reinforcing seems very attractive. It is certainly the case that learning usually occurs when subjects are given right/wrong KR, and if we extend the reinforcement principle to secondary or symbolic reinforcement we appear to have a fairly direct analogy with primary and secondary reinforcement in animal learning. Yet on further analysis any straightforward attempt to apply the Law of Effect breaks down. The manipulation of additional rewards and punishments produces at best side effects on learning style and there is no direct evidence for the operation of a drive reduction mechanism. In a revised version the Law of Effect is immune to this criticism. The effects of instruction to learn, as illustrated by the ingenious experiments of Wallach and Henle and of Nuttin, are far more damaging to reinforcement as a simple biological principle. The reinforcement principle is not too sensitive to evidence showing that delays do not have the effect which might be expected, but it is necessary to involve a bridging principle (such as belongingness) to account for the ineffectiveness of learning delays. The strongest evidence for the simple principle of reinforcement is the spread of effect phenomenon but this has been shown to be open to a number of possible artifacts in measuring the effect and is susceptible to at least one plausible alternative explanation, the guessing sequence hypothesis. In the next chapter we shall examine the informative aspects of KR and further flaws in the principle of reinforcement will emerge.

7 Information

In the two preceding chapters we have been discussing two kinds of 'motivational' effects of KR, incentive or drive-inducing effects and reinforcing or drive-reducing effects. We now turn to the question: does KR have an 'informative' effect, and, if so, what is its nature and can it be distinguished from motivational effects, or alternately can motivational effects be 'reduced' to information or vice versa? Writing on the 'information versus effect' controversy in 1947, Postman observed 'Information is a concept which does not readily lend itself to experimental analysis.' Only two years later, Shannon and Weaver (1949) published *The Mathematical Theory of Communication*, and in a very short time the implications for psychology of a method of defining and measuring information began to be apparent. In the Shannon–Weaver theory, information is equated with the reduction of uncertainty. Prior to a message being received the potential recipient is uncertain as to what the message will be, but when he has received it the uncertainty is reduced or eliminated and the information is said to have been transmitted. The convenient metric for information is the *bit* unit. One bit of information is that which reduces prior uncertainty by half. Thus if someone is asked to guess a card drawn from a pack but is also told it is red, exactly half the possibilities are ruled out by this one bit of information.

Most of the applications have been in the area of skilled performance where rate of information transmission (in bits per second) has been a convenient measure for combining speed and accuracy in a variety of situations. Information theory has been applied less frequently to learning problems despite the fact that the teaching/learning situation might be said to be the prototype of all information transmission systems. No doubt learning theorists are reasonably satisfied with the concepts (such as reinforcement) they already have and show no special enthusiasm for the new concepts and techniques. There is, however, no difficulty in considering the learner, prior to getting KR, as in a state of uncertainty about the outcome of his response and the provision of KR as giving information and reducing uncertainty, for this is purely a matter of definition. Uncertainty does not have to be interpreted as a subjective conscious state for we can use the same formula to talk about such inanimate objects as telephone or radio systems or even two machines linked by a communication channel. In a mechanical or electronic system we know that information has been transmitted because the state of the 'receiver' is systematically altered by messages sent; so also in the human subject we know the information has been received by virtue of the altered behaviour of the learner.

One of the most important insights provided by information theory is that if we look at stimuli as messages, the information they convey is not so much a function of the nature of the stimuli themselves as what other stimuli *might* have occurred. Thus the informative value of any piece of KR is going to depend on how many different kinds of KR might have been sent as a result of a response. The KR used by Thorndike consisted typically of only two possible messages 'right' or 'wrong', but this does not mean to say that uncertainty concerning the correct response is always reduced by half for this is only so when two results are equiprobable. If the two results occur in unequal frequencies, e.g. if wrong is more likely than right on average, less than one bit per response will be transmitted. If we envisage a paired-associate item with four alternative answers, the KR 'right' would eliminate all uncertainty but 'wrong' would only rule out one of the four possibilities. Subjects will on average have to make two responses to identify the correct choice. Where the response is one of a variety of possibilities as in an open-ended paired-associate task or the line-drawing experiment, the KR 'wrong' conveys very little information indeed. It is not too surprising that 'punishments' have been found rather less effective than 'rewards' in this type of experiment. Thus there is no difficulty in talking about KR as information and, moreover, there is a convenient measure of information which can be simply determined by the relative frequencies of different possible results. In fact, information is now easier to define and measure than reward. Having in earlier chapters considered experimental attempts to manipulate reward independently of the informative function of KR, we now consider the alternative strategy of varying the kinds and amounts of information given in KR.

In a classic experiment, Trowbridge and Cason (1932) repeated Thorndike's line-drawing experiment with the addition of more detailed KR. Four groups of ten subjects each drew 100 lines in one of four conditions. The first was a control group with no KR, the second heard the experimenter speak a nonsense syllable after each response, a third group were given right/wrong information, right being defined as any response within an eighth of an inch on either side of the target, and the fourth group were provided with KR in deviations of an eighth of an inch from the target such as 'three-eighths too long', etc. The control and nonsense syllable groups did not show any indication of systematic learning but both informed groups did, the group receiving detailed directional information learning more than the right/wrong group. Similar results were obtained by Waters (1933) who had subjects estimate the duration of a twelve-second time interval by the reproduction method. The efficiency of learning was found to be related to the specificity of the information given.

The positioning task is a convenient one for the study of the informative properties of KR since the actual distance moved by the subject can be represented in various ways. Bilodeau (1966) gave a very thorough survey of this work

but some representative studies will be described her
The size of the correct target area and the size of the err
gradations can be varied and subjected to a number
systematic or non-systematic transformations. The que
tion can then be asked, how do learning and retention va
with different kinds and amounts of information, as, f
example, in the Trowbridge and Cason experiment whe
not only more precise information but also direction
information was given?

A series of studies done for the American Air Force ha
found little advantage in increased specificity of K R wi
lever positioning, rudder control and knob rotation task
Green, Zimilies and Spragg (1955), using knob rotatio
in which *S* has to bisect a known angle, found no diffe
ence between three-category K R (i.e. 'correct', 'too far
'not enough') and K R precise to the nearest degree althoug
the target area was the same in both cases. Both group
were superior to a no-K R control group.

The results of a lever positioning experiment carried ou
by Bilodeau (1952a) gave 'little support for the notion tha
differences in response precision required for matchin
(target response) was of consequence.' The subject pulls
lever and after five seconds one of a vertical display c
lamps is lighted indicating the extent of the movemen
in relation to the desired movement. Three degrees c
accuracy required to score a 'hit' were used. No difference
were found among the three groups over twelve learnin
trials and seven subsequent test trials.

A second study (Bilodeau, 1952b) compared true wid
and narrow targets with fake wide targets. These looke
like bigger targets but the precision required to score a hi
was in fact the same as the standard wide target. Again n
differences were found. The results are in agreement wit
Gagné's (1950) study using the rudder control test. Th
display is lateral and positioning is done with the fee
Other studies by Bilodeau (1953) and Bilodeau and Rosen
bach (1953) employed knob rotation, the first with syste
matically distorted K R and the second with 'rounded' erro

feedback. Subjects attempted the knob setting with a known score for the correct setting. In the first experiment the K R was systematically distorted for one group such that errors were reported more accurately the nearer the response to the target and larger errors were exaggerated according to a sliding scale. K R accuracy was related to the initial rate of learning, but after sixteen trials subjects with distorted K R had become almost as accurate as those with undistorted K R. Whilst this method gave greater K R accuracy for greater response accuracy, it also introduced inequality of scale units and it appeared that subjects took some time to learn that the scale units were unequal. When they discovered this their performance became as good as those with undistorted K R. In the second knob rotation study K R scores were 'rounded' to varying degrees. In seven groups one received K R accurate to the nearest 0·5 per cent of the target magnitude (a score of 200) and other groups were given less accurate K R up to the seventh group which had K R accurate only to the nearest 25 per cent. Whilst the two groups with the largest 'rounding error' learned slightly more slowly initially, by the seventh trial differences between all groups were negligible.

A study by Annett (1959) provides data on K R precision in relation to both training and non-K R transfer trials. Ten subjects in each of the three groups were given ten training trials with K R in a lever pulling task. The required distance was 60 mm and subjects were given K R after each attempt. One group received K R on a three-point scale, 'correct' being 60 mm $\pm$ 20 mm (i.e. three 40 mm categories). The second group had K R on a seven-point scale, and the third on a sixty-point scale which was accurate to the nearest 2 mm. After training, subjects carried straight on for a hundred retention trials with no K R. The group receiving the most precise K R appeared to approach the target score a little sooner than the other groups. There were no significant differences in rate or extent of learning over ten trials. Performance of all groups levelled off by the fourth trial, that is, after the third result.

On the retention trials the groups were significantly differ ent, those with the least precise K R being the most accurat and those with the medium precision being the worst. Th medium and fine tolerance groups tended to overestimat and the wide tolerance groups to underestimate. That a groups improved in the learning trials at about the sam rate and to the same extent is of interest. It appeared tha most subjects attempted to 'bracket' the target by succes sive approximations. In the pure case of bracketing sub jects would acquire one bit of information per tria regardless of the number of possible results. This is rational strategy when the units of K R are not know absolutely. It is of interest, but perhaps coincidental, tha most learning occurred in the first three trials, indicatin that the subjects could gain up to three bits of informatio at the rate of one bit per trial which is about what on would expect if subjects were making absolute judgement of kinaesthetic extent.

It seems, then, that in these unidimensional positionin, tasks subjects can make use of more information tha simply the binary right/wrong, but at the same time the do not extract much more than one bit per trial even whe provided with a greater amount of information. What i especially significant, however, is the fact that error in formation appears to be used in the most strategic way t hunt for the location of the unseen target. Error informa tion does not simply inhibit individual wrong response but has a positive effect in directing the subject's nex response.

In many tasks the subject could be wrong in man different ways and thus could be given extremely comple K R. Limitations on the amount of information the subjec can process suggests that learning by K R alone might be slow job. A few examples of tasks more complex tha positioning bear out this conclusion. Crafts and Gilber (1935) in a maze learning experiment gave error scores o varying complexity. It was found that more complex erro scores had little advantage over simple error scores, sub jects tending to get confused with the greater detail and in some cases preferred to ignore it. In multi-dimensional threshold tasks, Eriksen (1958) gave KR relevant to the dimensions of size, brightness, hue and combinations of these. KR had relatively little effect with the less discriminable dimensions over a long series of judgements. Brown (1910), studying the effects of KR on the estimation of differences between lifted weights, found that errors in judging large differences were reduced but not errors in judging small differences. In an experiment on computer-controlled training of complex sound recognition in which each sound varied in five ways each with five different values, Swets and Sewall (1963) found that subjects given KR relevant to each of the five dimensions (they were in fact given a choice between several teaching modes of which detailed KR was one) did less well than those who chose to observe the sounds and be told their names. These examples indicate that, although KR which is more specific than simply right and wrong can be used, the upper limit in the amount of information that it is worthwhile providing for a given response is soon reached.

Learning without KR

Another way in which the amount of information given in KR has been systematically varied is by withholding it on some trials. We can begin with the extreme case where no extrinsic KR is given at all. It would seem to be impossible for anyone to learn one of Thorndike's guessing tasks without KR, but in motor tasks with intrinsic KR the absence of augmented KR will not necessarily prevent all kinds of learning.

Seashore and Bavelas (1941) re-examined Thorndike's line drawing data and found evidence of some 'learning'. It is true that the subjects did not improve with respect to the experimenter's criterion of a four-inch line, but an increase in consistency of successive responses was noticed. Whatever length of line the subjects did produce they

tended to do it more systematically on the basis of th
limited kinaesthetic feedback available to them.

Tracking tasks also contain intrinsic feedback withou
which the subject could not track at all. Sackett (1947), fo
example, provided augmented K R (time on target scores
and found little advantage over the no-K R condition
Others such as Smode (1958) have found difference
favouring augmented K R. The advantage probably de
pends on how good the intrinsic K R in the task is and th
extent to which the subject's criteria of good performanc
corresponds to that of the experimenter. One subject ma
track closely behind the target just out of toleranc
whilst another may choose to see how often he can hit o
cross it. These two performances would give very differen
results depending on whether *E* used time on target, roo
mean square error or some other criterion. Extrinsic K R i
only essential for learning what the *experimenter* regard
as good performance.

Reference has already been made in chapter 3 t
cases where subjects apparently improve the accurac
of perceptual judgements by sheer repeated experience t
the stimulus material. These studies were reviewed b
Eleanor Gibson (1953). The Poggendorff illusion wa
studied by Judd (1902) and by Cameron and Steele (1905
who found repeated experience reduced the illusion. Judd
who acted as one of his own subjects, reported, 'The illu
sion disappears after practice. It disappears not by any
process of judgement or any process of indirect correction
The line comes to look differently than it did at first'. O
course, Judd and probably his other subjects knew th
nature of the illusion before they started, but it is less easy
to dismiss the results of more objective studies, such as th
finding by Wolfe (1923) that subjects would improve th
accuracy with which they bisected lines by up to 25 pe
cent without K R, or even Judd's own experiment in plac
ing dots on an imagined extension to a line (about 7 pe
cent improvement). Others such as Moers (1924) and
Hamilton (1929) were not quite so successful. More re-

cently Eriksen (1958) found some support for the hypothesis that repeated exposure to a series of seventeen to twenty stimulus items each repeated 100 times did improve absolute thresholds for size, brightness, size and brightness, brightness and hue, and size, brightness and hue. Some subjects had K R for the first seventy-four judgements and others only for the first eight judgements. In the three-dimensional judgements 'corrected' and 'uncorrected' groups performed almost as well, but this seems partly due to the likelihood that the corrected group did not make very good use of the very detailed K R they were given. Nevertheless, there is a residual core of evidence that genuine improvement occurs without K R; possibly repeated experience permits subjects to build up some internal form of response against which to judge new instances – an hypothesis proposed by Johnson (1944, 1946 and 1949). In general we may conclude that subjects may be capable of 'learning' a variety of skills without formal extrinsic K R but they are most unlikely to learn what the experimenter has in mind as a performance criterion unless he lets them know.

Partial K R

If the analogy between K R and reinforcement is inappropriate and the function of K R is best described in terms of the information it provides, then only those trials on which K R is given should contribute to learning and retention. With the absolute number of trials on which K R is given held constant, any number of additional non-K R trials should have no effect on learning and retention. In operant conditioning the effect of 'partial reinforcement' is to extend the number of trials required for extinction. Following the analogy a number of investigators have looked into the possibility of enhancing retention by giving 'partial K R'.

Some apparent support for the partial reinforcement hypothesis comes from a study of flexible gunnery training by Houston (1947). A training device consisting of a

mock-up machine gun and a moving target plane pro
jected on a screen was used. The device was arranged such
that when a 'hit' was scored a coloured filter dropped over
the target projector and the plane turned red. Verbal K R
was given. The 'filter' treatment, the 'scores' treatment and
a combination were all given under three conditions of
fixed-ratio periodic reinforcement, that is on every trial
(100 per cent), on every second trial (50 per cent), or on
every fourth trial (25 per cent). The filter plus scores at
100 per cent gave the best learning, but on transfer trials
without K R performance dropped sharply and immediately. This drop was far less dramatic in the case of the 50
per cent and 25 per cent 'reinforcement'. This looks rather
like the effect obtained in operant conditioning.

Morin and Gagné (1951), however, on the basis of their
own data in a similar experiment, and Miller (1953), reviewing these studies, suggest that the filter and scores
give an artificial boost to performance by providing more
cues for the subject to work with. When these are taken
away performance reaches a level one might expect had
these cues never been given. Under 'partial reinforcement'
conditions, the boost to performance is not so great and
hence the subsequent drop is less.

The standard study on the effects of omitting K R in
some trials is by Bilodeau and Bilodeau (1958a). The task
was to learn to pull a lever through an arc of some 33
degrees. K R was given to the nearest degree plus the words
'too high' or 'too low', since S was not told the value of the
'correct' arc. Four groups practised, one with K R after
every trial, a second with K R every third trial, a third with
K R every fourth trial and a fifth with K R every tenth trial.
Practice went on until all subjects had had ten trials with
K R. The amount of error in the ten trials immediately
following each K R trial was found to be approximately
equal for all groups. The amount of learning was therefore
related to the absolute rather than the relative frequency of
K R. No evidence could be found of any improvement on
trials after those immediately following K R. It is unfor-

tunate that no study was made of performance subsequent to the complete and final removal of K R. The result would be of interest since to find no difference would sharply contradict the evidence from the conditioning studies. If a difference were to be found there would be a nice problem about the nature of the contribution of the non-K R trials, it already having been demonstrated that 'nothing' is learnt.

In tasks more closely resembling operant conditioning, classical 'partial reinforcement effects' can be found. Phares (1957) and James and Rotter (1958) have used tasks in which S is asked to bet on his future performance at difficult or impossible tasks with varying amounts of re-inforcement. The tasks were done under either chance or skill conditions, with instructions so phrased that S be-lieved his results were either due to his own skill or due to external chance factors. Phares used two difficult tasks, one of matching colours and another of matching lines of similar length and distributed 'reinforcement' in a prearranged arbitrary manner. The subjects' expectancy of success changed considerably according to the reinforcement schedule under the skill condition but not under the chance condition. James and Rotter using an impossible task in which S had to guess whether a series of cards would bear an O or an X managed to persuade naïve students in one group that success was related to skill. The response to be learnt and extinguished was a high expectancy of success at the task. One group received 100 per cent reinforcement and another 50 per cent, each being equally divided between the skill and chance conditions. The latter pro-duced results typical of partial reinforcement in condition-ing experiments, but under skill conditions 100 per cent reinforcement was slightly but not significantly, slower to extinguish than 50 per cent reinforcement.

Blank Trials

The general rule that trials on which no K R is given have no effect on learning is apparently contradicted by some recent work in concept information. In learning task where the subject may be told 'right' or 'wrong', one o' both of these results may be omitted. Thus the subjec can be told 'right' or 'wrong', 'nothing' or 'wrong', o' 'nothing' or 'right' (Buchwald, 1959a and b; Buss, Braden Orgel and Buss, 1956; Buss and Buss, 1956) or can be given right or wrong information on some trials but nothing on others (Bourne, Guy and Wadsworth, 1967; Bourne and Pendleton, 1958; Gormezano and Grant, 1958; Levine Leitenberg and Richter, 1964; Moore and Halpern, 1967) The evidence suggests that, for these tasks at least, a 'blank' trial is not neutral but more like 'right' and that the combinations 'right or wrong' and 'nothing or wrong' are not equivalent to 'nothing or right'.

Buss and Buss (1956) and Buss *et al.* (1956) used the materials for the Wisconsin Card Sorting Test which consists of cards bearing different geometric forms varying in colour and also in the number of forms per card. The subjects had to learn to sort these first by shape and then by colour independently of other dimensions. After each card was sorted subjects were either given 'right or wrong', 'nothing or wrong' or 'nothing or right' information. Taking the number of trials to a criterion of ten successive correct sortings, it was found that the combination 'right or nothing' resulted in much slower learning than either 'right or wrong' or 'nothing or wrong'. Buss and Buss suggest that, provided one makes the assumption that 'right' is only a weak positive reinforcer whereas 'wrong' is a very much stronger negative reinforcer, this curious result could be consistent with a reinforcement theory of learning. From this one could predict that any combination of results containing 'wrong' would lead to faster learning. Whilst this explanation fits the immediate facts, the assumptions are questionable. The weight of evidence from other studies (accepting the reinforcement view) is quite the reverse, that is to say, 'right' is a strong positive reinforcer whilst 'wrong' is either neutral or slightly positively reinforcing. Thorndike's explanation of the spread of effect is based on these assumptions (Thorndike, 1933a) and most other reinforcement theorists have argued that reward is generally more effective than punishment. Buchwald (1959a and b) from rather similar findings argued that the no-KR result acquired certain value by virtue of its pairing with 'right' or 'wrong'. Thus when paired with 'right' no-KR (nothing or right) acquires negative reinforcing value but when paired with 'wrong' (nothing or wrong) it acquires positive reinforcing value and, further, no-KR acquires greater positive reinforcing value in the 'nothing or wrong' condition. The result also presents a challenge to the point of view that KR is informative. Bourne, Guy and Wadsworth (1967) point out that, in the 'right or wrong', 'nothing or right' and 'nothing or wrong' procedures in concept learning experiments, the informative value of results depends not simply on the number of possible results (two), but on the proportions in which they occur, a point first made by Tilton (1939) in connexion with paired-associate learning. In the Buss studies there were more ways of being wrong than of being right, thus in the 'nothing or right' condition the subjects would get fewer trials with KR than in the 'nothing or wrong' condition and the trials-to-criterion measure used by Buss and Buss is therefore inappropriate. By systematically varying the proportions of trials in which 'right', 'wrong' and no-KR were given, Bourne and his co-workers were able to reproduce the earlier results in terms of trials-to-criterion, and also to show that when the number of trials accompanied by KR (either right or wrong) is held constant, differences between the 'right or wrong', 'right or nothing' and 'nothing or wrong' conditions disappear.

In both concept learning and paired-associate learning the number of ways of being wrong is clearly a factor to be taken into account, but asymmetrical effects of right and wrong have been found in certain types of two-alternative choice tasks. Levine, Leitenberg and Richter (1964) used a task in which pairs of nonsense syllables are presented and *S* is asked to choose one and is then told that his choice was right or wrong. A second card containing the same pair is then presented and a choice is required. The experiments consist of presenting ninety such pairs in succession and the rules determining the correct responses are changed. For example, the syllable which was right on the first trial might always be right on the second or might be always wrong, or the syllable which was right on the first trial could be wrong on 80 per cent of second trials or right on 80 per cent of second trials. The experiment is rather like the 'learning set' situation in which the subject is not learning which is the correct syllable but is learning the rule by which the correct syllable is determined. After a few pairs of presentations the subject is given a series of trials in which he is given no-KR but is told to go on trying to make correct guesses. If no-KR is neutral then the subjects might be expected, on the second presentation, to repeat their guesses about half the time and change their guesses for the other half. In fact the probability of repeat responses was found to be related to the probability of reversal in the training trials. On the face of it this result could be interpreted as meaning that no-KR was equivalent to 'right'. Levine *et al.* refer to this as the 'blank trials law' and adopt the position that blank trials are equivalent to positive reinforcement. This apparent equivalence is difficult to assimilate to conventional reinforcement theory but might be satisfactorily explained by reference to the subject's hypotheses. Both the result 'right' and no-KR give no indication to the subject that he should change his choice, his hypothesis concerning which of the two syllables is 'correct', whereas the result 'wrong' infirms the original hypothesis and stimulates a change of response. Thus, if we envisage the subject's choices as being mediated by an hypothesis and both 'right' and no-KR produce the same effects on the hypothesis, it remains unchanged.

What can we conclude from the effects of blank trials and no-KR on learning? It is clear that straightforward reinforcement interpretations lead to some paradoxical conclusions and some *ad hoc* adjustments to the value of positive and negative reinforcers. It is much easier to account for these results if K R is regarded as having simply an informative value. When appropriate corrections are made for the informational asymmetry of right and wrong results and if we allow that subjects can have a strategy for dealing with information, we no longer need to make *ad hoc* appeals to differences in the strength of positive and negative reinforcers.

Guidance

If we look at knowledge of results as providing feedback information which is essential for learning, the question must arise – is there any other way of giving the necessary information *without presenting it only as a consequence of action*? If, for example, the task is to learn to make a simple response to one of two alternative stimuli, the teacher might either let the learner try and then give him the knowledge of results (that was the right one) or he might indicate *before* the trial which response is correct. All existing versions of the reinforcement model appear to require that a response is made and that the after-effects of the response alone reinforce the behaviour or the s–r connexions. In many tasks an information model would be indifferent to the time of arrival of the relevant information. In any learning situation involving more than one trial, the result coming after any one response also comes before the next. There is no reason in principle why one should not envisage a model which stresses the pro-active effect of information on the next response, whether or not there has been a previous response, since *only in certain circumstances will the nature of the previous response be relevant*.

Techniques for providing advance information have been called variously *guidance* (Carr, 1930), *action feedback* (Miller, 1953), *prompting* and *cuing* and, according to the nature of the task to be learned and the species of the learner, these have taken a variety of forms. These can be classified into three main sets of methods:

(a) Forced response, sometimes called mechanical guidance which, in the case of motor skills involves literally putting the learner through the correct motions.

(b) Visual guidance which involves supplementary information, not contingent upon previous responses, which enables the learner to perform the required act more readily. This is often called cuing or action feedback.

(c) Verbal guidance which consists of telling the subject what to do or directly prompting the correct response (e.g. in paired-associate learning).

One of the earliest users of forced response was, curiously enough, Thorndike himself (1898) but apparently with little success. Thorndike's failure may have been due to the use of an inadequate technique (anyone who has attempted to force a cat to do something by holding it in the right position will appreciate the difficulty). Working with other species and other techniques later investigators obtained much better results. Cole (1907) using racoons in Thorndike-type puzzle box situations was able to teach them how to undo the latch by manually guiding their paws. Not only did these animals learn faster than by trial-and-error but some who had failed by that method were successfully taught by mechanical guidance.

The work of Carr (1930) and his co-workers (Alonzo, 1926; Koch, 1930; Ludgate, 1923; Waters, 1930 and Wang, 1925) has already been mentioned in chapter 4. In some cases blind alleys were blocked up and in other cases the rat was guided through the correct path manually or by means of a leash. Thorndike himself had suggested placing the animal in a trolley car and pulling it through the maze, but it was not until 1955 that Gleitman made successful use of this technique.

Carr, summarizing the Chicago guidance studies in 1930 (already described in chapter 4), concluded that guidance was an effective method and, under certain conditions, more effective than trial-and-error learning. The conditions principally concern the amount of guidance given. Clearly the amount of learning cannot be tested during guided trials so tests of effectiveness must be in terms of transfer to unguided trials. Typically the animals would be given a small number of trials, say five or ten, and the efficiency of these would be tested by the savings method, that is the number of trials of free practice still required for learning. In a typical result, twenty-five trials, the first five under mechanical guidance followed by a further twenty free trials, was as effective as thirty free trials. As measured by the savings method, the efficiency tended to decrease with the amount of guidance given, the most efficient combination being a small number of guided trials early in practice. Waters (1930) questioned this method of assessing guidance and, in experiments on human maze learning, concluded that any number of guided trials can be shown to have a beneficial effect in the sense of cutting down the number of unguided transfer trials needed to reach criterion. Waters also contributed the finding that guidance was superior on a one-week retention test.

Although these results seem to show that learning does not have to depend solely on obtaining the results of overt practice, questions can be raised about the information needed to perform the task and the way it is provided by guidance. Depending on the type of guidance and the type of task, there clearly can be considerable differences between the types of response made and the stimuli present during practice runs. If Thorndike's cats failed to learn it may have been that they were responding to the experimenter's manipulations. Similarly, any form of mechanical guidance creates a set of extraneous stimuli to which the subject may respond. The trolley car ride is perhaps the nearest thing to obtaining information about the result of an action without having to go through that action and even this is not a pure case.

The same kind of problem arises with other forms of forced response or mechanical guidance such as the tracking studies by Lincoln (1954, 1956), Bilodeau and Bilodeau

(1958), Holding (1959), Holding and McCrae (1964) and Gordon (1968). In Lincoln's studies the task was to learn to turn a handwheel at a standard rate with different forms of K R and guidance. Lincoln argued that to learn a rotation rate the subject must learn to rely on kinaesthetic cues. He compared learning by verbal K R with having the subject rest his hand on the wheel whilst it was rotated at the correct rate; in a third condition, the subject passively held the handle whilst it was rotated at a rate equivalent to the average error in the previous active trial, thus giving kinaesthetic error information. Learning was initially faster under the forced correct response conditions but only for the first ten trials when learning eventually ceased. Both verbal error information and kinaesthetic error information were superior in later practice and retention.

Holding (1959) used a visual tracking task which permitted subjects to track normally or to hold the actual control knob whilst it automatically traced out the correct path. In this case both guided and unguided learning quickly reached a maximum which was equivalent for both groups. Thus, both the techniques were about equally efficient, and, moreover, transfer between the two tasks was about equal.

I. Mc. D. Bilodeau and E. A. Bilodeau (1958) used a tracking task in which could be mechanically restricted by having the subjects' pointer run along the correct path in a groove. In the unrestricted condition the same course was followed but with the pointer running over a flush surface. After four training sessions subjects transferred from restricted to conventional tracking and vice versa. Both restricted and unrestricted practice were found to be beneficial and about equal in effect. In a very recent study (Gordon, 1968) using a rotary pursuit task, three conditions were compared, single tracking, mechanically restricted tracking, in which the subject chased the target by means of a stylus in a groove which permitted only lead and lag errors, and an augmented feedback condition in which a yellow light illuminated the field when S was on target. Mechanical guidance produced faster initial learning but poorer transfer to the unguided task. Although there are variations between the results of these studies it does seem that forced correct responding has some benefit, initially equivalent to or superior to unguided trials but that this advantage tends to disappear as practice progresses. From these researches one might suspect that differences between guided and unguided trials found in transfer may well have something to do with the kinds of cues available to subjects and the way they use them. There are most probably differences in the kinaesthetic stimulation between actually turning a handle and passively resting on it whilst it is turned. The problem is that we are left speculating for, if the detailed cue structure of the task is important in this kind of way, we have yet to develop methods of studying it.

This particular problem does not occur with the second type of guidance, referred to by Holding as visual guidance. Although most examples are in fact visual, guidance could, in principle, be given by any modality; the aim simply is to ensure correct performance by providing some additional cues which are not present in the standard task. R. B. Miller coined the term 'action feedback' (although it is not strictly speaking feedback at all) to describe this addition of cues which can support correct performance. It is worthwhile distinguishing this from augmented feedback which is also an additional cue, such as the yellow light in Gordon's study and the red filter and the check sight and buzzer of the gunnery studies described earlier. In these cases the extra cue is feedback in the strict sense of being dependent on prior or current performance. Holding's visual guidance or Miller's action feedback is functionally the same as the third category, verbal guidance, or the equivalent terms of prompting (used mostly in verbal learning) and cuing (used mostly in perceptual and motor learning). The common ground of all is that they provide information on which S can base his next response and that this information is quite independent of previous responses. The important difference between action feedback/prompting/cuing and the mechanical forms of guidance is that there is no difference in the physical characteristics of the response due to guidance and that there are no additional cues generated by the restrictions of mechanical guidance. What additional cues are present are under the experimenter's control. The action feedback situation is therefore much more convenient for looking at the questions related to the kind of information the subject is given and its relationship (especially temporal relationships) to the responses produced.

One of the most dramatic examples of visual guidance, von Wright's (1957) maze learning experiment has already been described in chapter 4. It will be recalled that subjects learning a series of binary choices reached criterion in many fewer trials when they were permitted to see the outcome of each binary choice just prior to making a decision. This rather striking example of the superiority of guidance or action feedback compared with trial and error does strongly suggest that, in some tasks at least, it may be possible to present information which the subject needs for learning in a more efficient way than by simply giving KR. The situations where this is not so are those in which a response is necessary in order to extract information from the environment. Manual tasks depending mainly on kinaesthetic information are clearly in this category. Von Wright's maze is not primarily a manual task since it consists of learning a series of binary choices, which can be quite readily coded in verbal form. Following this line of reasoning one would expect that other verbal tasks (such as paired-associate learning) and perceptual tasks (such as identification and discrimination) could be as readily taught by cuing and prompting methods as by knowledge of results; indeed this does seem to be the case, as we have seen in earlier chapters. The general conclusion of verbal learning studies is that prompting is normally equal to and sometimes superior to KR and the same appears to be true of perceptual identification and discrimination. Where K R is at a disadvantage mainly appears to be due to the delay between the stimulus and the K R being usually greater than is the case of cuing or prompting. This has certainly been found in the case of auditory detection and recognition by Swets and Sewall (1963) and by Annett and Paterson (1966, 1967) who conclude that the identification of authenticated samples of the signal to be detected seems to be the principal requirement for learning.

To summarize, the once popular view that it is what happens after a response that matters must be modified in the light of evidence which has been accumulating in recent years. We sometimes forget that the information provided by K R comes between responses; the fact that it comes before one response may be as important, if not more important, than the fact that it comes after the previous response. Several types of guidance, cuing and prompting have been described. Mechanical guidance, physically preventing errors, is a moderately effective technique but transfer to unguided trials is often less than perfect. Non-mechanical forms of guidance or prompting are, however, at least as effective and sometimes more effective than trial and error. Motor tasks in which kinaesthetic information is important require a response as the necessary means of acquiring this information, but in both verbal and perceptual tasks where information need not be dependent on responses, cuing and prompting techniques are as efficient and sometimes more efficient. It is possible that K R methods only serve to delay or complicate the relationship between the stimulus and the response term and to this extent are less efficient. The evidence suggests that the emphasis on results as such is misplaced, although there are some situations where the necessary information can be gained only as a result of a response.

8 Conclusion

A detailed summary of the empirical findings on KR will not be attempted in this final chapter but rather we shall concentrate on the main theoretical outcomes of the evidence and the arguments presented. We began in chapter 1 by giving a broad outline of the concept of feedback as it appears to be applicable to behaviour. The next three chapters summarized some of the main lines of empirical investigations of KR, whilst chapters 5, 6 and 7 examined the theoretical basis of what are believed to be the principal functions of KR, namely as incentive, reinforcement and information. The first two 'motivational' functions have always been difficult to reconcile with the 'informative' function and so, having adopted the 'informational' feedback approach, our main task has been to show that all the supposedly different functions of KR can be derived from the properties of feedback systems without recourse to a 'mixed' (i.e. motivational-cum-informational) theory.

To say that KR has an incentive function adds nothing to its properties as feedback since in a general sense 'motivation' can be regarded as feedback in action. There would seem to be no difference in principle between a servo 'hunting' for a specified set of goal conditions and an animal in search of food or indeed any organism indulging in 'goal-directed' activity. In incentive experiments KR generally has two roles. First, as feedback, it is essential to the attainment of some target performance, and second, given no other statement of the goal, KR in certain forms can be taken as implying a goal, that is as a supplementary form of 'instructions'. This position would seem to be consistent with the evidence, some of which is rather puzzling in terms of any conventional motivation theory.

Next we looked in detail at KR as reinforcement. Although the basic principle of reinforcement or effect bears a number of different interpretations (some of which are rather hard to tie down), it has serious empirical and theoretical defects which cannot be lightly brushed aside. First, let us briefly summarize the principal failures of reinforcement theory to deal with the empirical evidence. We found that stimuli which would normally be regarded as being rewarding and punishing did not always have the predicted effects. Adding financial bonuses or electric shocks to informative K R appears to have only marginal and indirect effects on learning efficiency in human subjects, but this evidence militates against only a rather crude and simple-minded version of reinforcement theory. The defect can be repaired by invoking either the concept of secondary reinforcement or something like Thorndike's 'O K reaction'. Such a shift, whilst coping with this direct criticism, constitutes a fundamental change in the reinforcement principle. In the first place, either concept represents an additional hypothesis rather than an explanation, but the more fundamental change is that reinforcement is now at least one stage removed from the underlying motivation or drive-reduction principle. In either case the reinforcement principle takes a big step towards an informational concept since the actual K R is seen as an indicator or signal rather than something which directly reduces drive; in fact the drive reduction process is entirely inferential. Another set of evidence inimical to the reinforcement principle is the relative immunity of K R to temporal delays. Here again, some symbolic mediating process must be invoked to account for the maintenance of an S–R link until such time as the K R arrives to reinforce the link. Thorndike invoked the concept of 'belongingness', but in doing so took yet another step away from reinforcement as an immediate, automatic 'biological' principle. The main evidence that reinforcement does operate in this simple and immediate fashion comes from the phenomenon of 'spread of effect'; yet, as we have seen, the phenomenon is only exhibited in certain limited types of guessing situation and its existence independently of the operation of any guessing strategies and measurement artifacts is seriously in doubt.

The strongest empirical evidence against a straightforward principle of reinforcement comes from the apparent failure of reinforcers under certain conditions of instruction to learn. The results obtained by Wallach and Henle and by Nuttin in a variety of simple learning experiments are difficult to assimilate to any version of reinforcement theory, even one which relies only on secondary reinforcement or the hypothetical O K reaction. The tasks used by these investigators are precisely those in which the effects of reinforcers should be automatic and inevitable, and yet the results indicate that this is clearly not so. It is not possible to conceive a principle of reinforcement which is only *sometimes* automatic and so a single negative instance is damning.

The reinforcement principle has several critical, logical difficulties, one being the problem of defining reinforcers independently of their empirically reinforcing properties; but perhaps the most serious flaw lies in Thorndike's original derivation of the principle from his evidence. In experiments in which the subject is 'rewarded' by being told 'right' after correct responses he tends to learn these responses. In effect, Thorndike argued that rewards therefore caused learning, and at first sight this appears to be a perfectly reasonable conclusion from the evidence. However, a closer look suggests some logical flaws. Consider first the problem of what is meant by 'learning'. Suppose that in a Thorndike-type guessing task a subject had tended to repeat all responses beginning arbitrarily with the letter 'b' and that these were not, except occasionally by chance, the responses E had rewarded. An independent observer looking at the results but not knowing which responses E had rewarded might conclude that learning had taken place, but, from the experimenter's point of view, no learning had occurred. Which of them is right? Well, clearly it depends on how 'learning' is defined. The independent observer is treating learning as any systematic change in behaviour whilst the experimenter is using a narrower definition to the effect that the change must be towards some previously specified behaviour. For convenience, let us call these two usages learning 1 and learning 2 respectively. In the case of learning 2 the behavioural change must be in the direction of some behaviour specified by a rule which the experimenter has in mind and by which he gives or withholds rewards or issues instructions. Now if E had no specification or rule in mind, learning 1 might still occur but learning 2, by definition, could not occur. Without a specification of correct responses there is, strictly speaking, no task to be learnt, and it follows that a rule defining correct responses is a prerequisite for learning 2.

Now it is clearly not enough that E should simply 'have in mind' the rule specifying 'correct' behaviour. If E never mentioned to the learner that responses X, Y and Z were correct and yet reliable evidence were to be found that S's behaviour was changing in this direction, we would conclude that some form of telepathy was being used. From the subject's point of view there is nothing to be learnt until correct and incorrect responses are specified: this would be true whatever the physiological mechanism of learning might be and whether the learner were a man, a rat or a computer. It is a prerequisite of learning 2 that some message conveys the specification of 'correct' responses and that it must pass from the teacher to the learner. A simple illustration may help show that this is a logical rather than a psychological point. Consider two separate rows of lights, A and B, which can be illuminated in arbitrary patterns. The two light patterns symbolize patterns of behaviour, that in row A the pattern which an E specifies as 'correct' and that in row B a subject's actual behaviour. The pattern of row A is fixed but the pattern of row B varies arbitrarily and any increase in correspondence between the two patterns can be thought of as an instance of learning 2. Now it is easy to see that whilst pattern B may from time to time fortuitously resemble pattern A, there can be no systematic correspondence between the two unless an information link is set up. A message representing the desired pattern must be transmitted from A to B. It does not matter how the message is sent or by what means the lamps in row B are made to conform to the pattern in row A. Whatever the physical nature of the mechanism an information link is logically required.

This line of argument leads to the conclusion that learning 2, that is learning in the sense used by Thorndike, depends on certain logical requirements which are quite independent of any specific psychological or physiological mechanisms. These are (a) that the 'correct' behaviour must be specified, and (b) that some message containing the specification must be transmitted to the learner. In tasks where the learner has no other means of finding out which are the correct responses knowledge of results is therefore a prerequisite for learning, but we should be careful to distinguish between a prerequisite and a cause. Thorndike appears to have mistaken a logical necessity for a biological fact, and was thus led to unwarranted conclusions about the role of effect and to pointless speculation about the underlying physiological processes and their relation to rewards and drives.

To conclude let us briefly sketch out the informative role of KR in learning, bearing in mind the basic principles outlined in chapter 1. KR is regarded as information about the outcome of a test carried out on the environment. The test generally depends on the subject's making a 'response', but not necessarily so. The essential implication of experimental results in guidance and prompting is that in many situations the subject can either make a response in order, for example, to find out which of two possibilities is 'right', or he can be told the outcome without having to make a response. The informative function of KR depends on two main factors, the nature of the information and what is done with it. By the nature of the information we mean, for example, how much information (in the information theory sense) is conveyed by the message. Thus a test may have two possible outcomes or many and we have seen that subjects can respond to different amounts of information. What the subject does with the information is determined by the transformation rule. This idea was introduced in chapter 1 but may need a little further explanation here. An elementary servo such as a thermostat has a very simple transformation rule such as 'when temperature exceeds x switch off the boiler, when temperature is below y switch on the boiler'. A more complex servo, such as an automatic tracking system, may have a more complex transformation rule (usually called the transfer function in this context) which translates data concerning, say the magnitude and error, rate of change of error, etc., into appropriate corrective action.

Simple positioning tasks illustrate how these concepts can be used. By varying the specificity or detail given in KR we are varying the information content of KR and by noting how the subject responds on successive learning trials we can get some idea of the nature of the transformation rule he is using. Clearly subjects' demonstrated ability to use more detailed information implies the existence of fairly complex transformation rules. We could look at the reinforcement principle as representing an hypothesis that subjects learn only on the basis of a very simple transformation rule which states roughly 'if good increase probability of preceding response, if bad decrease probability of preceding response'. Whilst such a rule *may* be used it is clear that this is not the *only one* and we must regard the human learner as in general capable of the use of more complex transformation rules in acquiring skills. The observed complexity of human learning seems to require the operation of a hierarchy of tests or a *plan* as suggested by Miller, Galanter and Pribram (1960). Figure 10 shows a purely hypothetical plan, or hierarchy of tests, by which a subject could conceivably deal with the problem of learning to draw a line to a specified length receiving simple directional KR. The algorithmic form is convenient be-

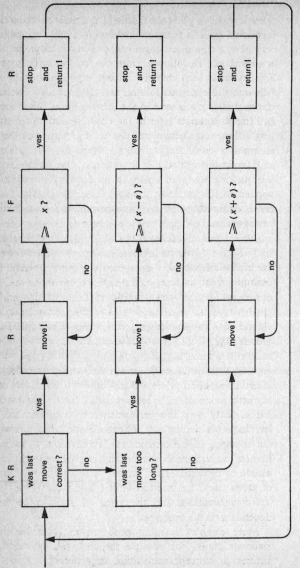

Figure 10 Algorithm for learning position skill

cause it makes explicit the nature of the tests and the transformation rules and because it shows in a quite compelling
way how such a mechanism could be made to work. The
arrows should be followed from the top left hand corner.
The layout is such that the information provided by K R
falls into the left hand column and the necessary intrinsic
(kinaesthetic) K R is seen in the third column. The second
and fourth columns refer to the response and its termina-
tion. All the transformation rules are represented as simple
alternatives depending on tests applied to both extrinsic
and intrinsic feedback. It is assumed that one response
x units long has been made. In the first column a test is
applied to the extrinsic K R and, depending on the outcome, either the next response commences or a further
test is made. The three rows represent three 'subroutines'
which are entered according to the outcomes of the initial
tests. Each subroutine involves a slightly different use of
the intrinsic feedback, a different transformation rule. For
example, frequent tests in the top row are made and the
movement is ended when, within the limits of kinaesthetic
sensitivity, it is equal to or greater than x whilst in the
second row the movement ends when it is equal to or
greater than x minus an arbitrary length a, and in the
third row when it is equal to or greater than $x + a$. A working model could be built or run on a computer with the
insertion of appropriate values for the accuracy of kinaesthetic judgement (for tests in the I F column) and would
mimic fairly well the performance of a human subject
learning a positioning task. The model can be refined without changing its basic structure. For example, in so far as
human subjects are to some extent responsive to the magnitude of reported error, further tests for the magnitude
of error could be inserted at the beginning of the two
'error' subroutines and the value of a could be made
dependent on the outcome.

More complex learning problems may involve more
elaborate plans. For example the strategies identified by
Bruner in concept acquisition experiments can be re-

garded as detailed plans for discovering the concept. The conservative focusing strategy, for example, would appear to involve a plan for which the first test identifies any positive instance of the concept the experimenter has in mind. Items are first chosen at random but the transformation rule applied to the test outcome 'correct' would be 'choose the next item such that it differs in only one respect from the preceding correct item' and so on. Hunt, Marin and Stone (1966) have described a number of problems solving algorithms. These examples are merely illustrative of the point that the informative value of K R depends not only on the K R itself but on the nature of the underlying plan by which the subject is attempting the solution of the learning problem.

Finally let us summarize the main conclusions. Except in the case of the reinforcement principle, the role of results or consequences in behaviour seems to have been underrated. Behaviour can be described in terms of hierarchies of feedback loops along the lines suggested by Miller, Galanter and Pribram and this emphasizes the crucial importance of 'results' at all levels of behaviour. The general feedback concept puts K R, as traditionally used, in its proper context. What is normally called K R involves the manipulation of an external feedback loop relating to certain aspects of a subject's performance. All tasks involve intrinsic feedback to a greater or lesser extent and externally provided K R must be understood in relation to this. A survey of motor, perceptual and verbal tasks shows that typically K R has different functions in each. The performance of motor skills in particular involves intrinsic K R, and, whilst without extrinsic K R subjects may not learn to achieve some specified standard of performance, learning is often possible on the basis of this intrinsic K R. A practical suggestion is that training devices should be used primarily to draw the trainee's attention to intrinsic K R. In many perceptual and verbal tasks K R has been used as the *only* means of providing a performance standard, that is specifying the nature of the task to be learnt, and to this extent K R is crucial to learning. Yet in verbal tasks it is often just as easy to tell the subjects 'the answer' and in perceptual tasks to demonstrate the stimulus. Various forms of prompting, cuing and guidance are efficient teaching techniques.

To say that K R 'provides motivation' is misleading. The so-called incentive function of K R seems to involve both providing the subject with a performance standard to aim for and information necessary for corrective action. Without a standard K R is useless, but the provision of a standard can lead to performance increments without additional extrinsic K R provided intrinsic K R is available. The mystery surrounding the incentive function, and in particular the apparent contradiction between the drive-inducing and drive-reducing functions of K R, is largely due to the varieties of meanings which have been attached to the word 'motivation'. It is suggested that we describe an organism as being 'motivated' when we see it apparently pursuing some plan of action. Since plans involve hierarchies of feedback loops, feedback is essential to motivation but motivation is not an additional energizing factor; it is simply descriptive of feedback in action.

The Law of Effect as the central principle of learning has been rejected on both empirical and logical grounds. The idea that K R is reinforcing is reducible to the hypothesis that learning plans only involve one simple transformation rule and this appears to be untrue in many learning situations where learners are demonstrably sensitive to different kinds and amounts of information. Some tentative suggestions have been made as to how the learning of even simple motor tasks could be described as the operation of learning plans, in principle similar to the 'strategies' found in problem-solving tasks. The use made of various kinds and amounts of K R information could tell us a lot about how these plans are organized. The informative value of K R is seen in terms not only of the information content of the 'results' but also in relation to the kind of transformation rule the learner is using.

The influence of cybernetics on psychological thinking in a variety of spheres is already profound. The systematic application of feedback principles to the familiar topic of knowledge of results could not have been long delayed and, if this book serves to clarify some old confusions and to suggest some ways of thinking and lines of investigation, a start will have been made.

References

Alexander, L. T. (1951), 'Knowledge of results and the temporal gradient of reinforcement', *Amer. Psychologist*, vol. 6, pp. 292–3.

Alonzo, A. S. (1926), 'The influence of manual guidance on maze learning', *J. comp. Psychol.*, vol. 6, pp. 143–57.

Amsel, A. (1960), 'Error responses and reinforcement schedules in self-instructional devices', in Lumsdaine, A. A., and Glaser, R. (eds.), *Teaching Machines and Programmed Learning: A Sourcebook*, DAVI-NEA, Washington, D.C.

Angell, G. W. (1949), 'The effect of immediate knowledge of quiz results on final examination scores in freshman chemistry', *J. educ. Res.*, vol. 42, pp. 391–4.

Annett, J. (1959), Unpublished Doctoral Thesis, Oxford University.

Annett, J. (1965), 'A low cost cheatproof teaching system', *Prog. Learning*, vol. 1, pp. 155–8.

Annett, J. (1966a), 'Payoff: a neglected factor in reaction time measurement', *Quart. J. exp. Psychol.*, vol. 18, pp. 273–4.

Annett, J. (1966b), 'Training for perceptual skills', *Ergonomics*, vol. 9, pp. 459–68.

Annett, J., and Clarkson, J. (1964), 'The use of cuing in training tasks', U.S. Navy Report, NAVTRADEVCEN 3143–1.

Annett, J., and Duncan, K.D. (1967), 'Task analysis and training design', *Occup. Psychol.*, vol. 41, pp. 211–21.

Annett, J., and Paterson, L. (1966), 'The use of cuing in training tasks: phase II', U.S. Navy Report, NAVTRADEVCEN 4119–1.

Annett, J., and Paterson, L. (1967), 'The use of cuing in

training tasks: phase III', U.S. Navy Report, N A V T R A-
D E V C E N 4717–1.

Arps, G. F. (1917), 'A preliminary report on work with
knowledge versus work without knowledge of results',
Psychol. Rev., vol. 24, pp. 449–53.

Attneave, F. (1959), *Applications of Information Theory
to Psychology*, Holt, Rinehart and Winston.

Bahrick, H. P., Fitts, P. M., and Rankin, R. E. (1952),
'Effect of incentives upon reaction to peripheral stimuli',
J. exp. Psychol., vol. 44, pp. 400–406.

Bain, A. (1868), *The Senses and the Intellect* (3rd edn),
Longmans Green.

Battig, W. F. (1954), 'The effect of kinaesthetic, verbal
and visual cues on the acquisition of a lever-positioning
skill', *J. exp. Psychol.*, vol. 47, p. 371.

Becker, J. L. (1964), 'The effect of withholding reinforcement in auto-instructional programs', in Ofiesh, G. D.,
and Meierhenry, W. C., *Trends in Programmed Instruction*, D A V I - N E A, N S P I, Washington.

Becker, P. W., Mussina, C. M., and Persons, R. W. (1963),
'Intertrial interval, delay of knowledge of results, and
motor performance', *Percept. mot. Skills*, vol. 17, pp.
559–63.

Bell, C. (1826), 'On the nervous circle which connects the
voluntary muscles with the brain', *Philos. Trans.*, pt 2,
pp. 163–73.

Bergum, B. O., and Klein, I. C. (1961), 'A survey and
analysis of vigilance research', H U M R R O *Res. Rep.*,
no. 8.

Bernard, J., and Gilbert, R. W. (1941), 'The specificity of
the effect of shock per error in a maze learning experiment with human subjects', *J. exp. Psychol.*, vol. 28,
pp. 178–86.

Biel, W. C., Brown, C. E., and Gottsdanker, R. (1944),
'The effectiveness of a check sight technique for training 40 mm gun pointers who are using the computing
sight M7', *O S R D Report* no. 4054, Appl. Psychol.
Panel, N D R C, Washington, D.C.

Bilodeau, E. A. (1951), 'Acquisition of skill on the Rudder Control Test with various forms of social competition', U S A F H R R C *Res.* Note, 52–6.

Bilodeau, E. A. (1952a), 'Some effects of various degrees of supplemented information given at two levels of practice upon the acquisition of a complex motor skill', U S A F H R R C *Res. Bull.*, 52–15.

Bilodeau, E. A. (1952b), 'A further study of the effects of target size and goal attainment upon the development of response accuracy', U S A F H R R C *Res. Bull.*, 52–7.

Bilodeau, E. A. (1953), 'Speed of acquiring a simple motor response as a function of the systematic transformation of K R', *Am. J. Psychol.*, vol. 66, pp. 409–20.

Bilodeau, E. A. (1966), 'Retention', in Bilodeau, E. A. (ed.), *Acquisition of Skill*, Academic Press, pp. 315–50.

Bilodeau, E. A., and Bilodeau, I. Mc. D. (1958a), 'Variable frequency of knowledge of results and the learning of a simple skill', *J. exp. Psychol.*, vol. 55, pp. 379–83.

Bilodeau, E. A., and Bilodeau, I. Mc. D. (1958b), 'Variation of temporal intervals among critical events in five studies of knowledge of results', *J. exp. Psychol.*, vol. 55, pp. 603–12.

Bilodeau, E. A., and Rosenbach, J. H. (1953), 'Acquisition of response proficiency as a function of rounding error in informative feedback', H R R C *Res. Bull.*, 53–21.

Bilodeau, E. A., and Ryan, F. J. (1960), 'A test for interaction of delay of knowledge of results and two types of interpolated activity', *J. exp. Psychol.*, vol. 59, pp. 414–19.

Bilodeau, I. Mc. D. (1966), 'Information feedback', in Bilodeau, E. A. (ed.), *Acquisition of Skill*, Academic Press, pp. 255–96.

Bilodeau, I. Mc D., and Bilodeau, E. A. (1958), 'Transfer of training and the physical restriction of response', *Percept. mot. Skills*, vol. 8, pp. 71–8.

Birmingham, H. P., and Taylor, F. V. (1954), 'A design philosophy for man–machine control systems', *Proc. I.R.E.*, vol. 42, no. 12.

Boersma, F. J. (1965), 'Effects of delay of information feedback and length of post-feedback interval on linear programmed learning', *Michigan State Univ. Diss. Abstr.*, vol. 26, p. 1180.

Bourne, L. E. (1966a), *Human Conceptual Behaviour*, Allyn and Bacon Inc.

Bourne, L. E. (1966b), 'Information feedback. Comments on Professor I.Mc.D. Bilodeau's paper', in Bilodeau, E. A. (ed.), *Acquisition of Skill*, Academic Press, ch. 6, pp. 297–313.

Bourne, L. E., and Bunderson, C. V. (1963), 'Effects of delay of informative feedback and length of post-feedback interval on concept identification', *J. exp. Psychol.*, vol. 65, pp. 1–5.

Bourne, L. E., Guy, D. E., and Wadsworth, N. (1967), 'Verbal reinforcement combinations and the relative frequency of informative feedback in a card sorting task', *J. exp. Psychol.*, vol. 73, pp. 220–26.

Bourne, L. E., and Pendleton, R. B. (1958), 'Concept identification as a function of completeness and probability of information feedback', *J. exp. Psychol.*, vol. 56, pp. 413–20.

Broadbent, D. E. (1958), *Perception and Communication*, Pergamon Press.

Broadbent, D. E., and Gregory, M. (1963), 'Vigilance considered as a statistical decision', *Brit. J. Psychol.*, vol. 54, pp. 309–23.

Brown, W. (1910), 'The judgment of difference with special reference to the doctrine of the threshold, in the case of lifted weights', *Univ. Calif. Publ. Psychol.*, vol. 1, p. 1.

Brown, I. D. (1966), 'An asymmetrical transfer effect in research on knowledge of performance', *J. appl. Psychol.*, vol. 50, pp. 118–20.

Bruner, J. S., Goodnow, J. J., and Austin, G. A. (1956), *A Study of Thinking*, Wiley.

Bryan, G. L., and Rigney, J. W. (1956), 'An evaluation of a method for shipboard training in operations knowledge', *Tech. Rep. Personnel and Training Board*, O N R, no. 18.

Buchwald, A. M. (1959a), 'Extinction after acquisition under different verbal reinforcement combinations', *J. exp. Psychol.*, vol. 57, pp. 43–8.

Buchwald, A. M. (1959b), 'Experimental alterations in the effectiveness of verbal reinforcement combinations', *J. exp. Psychol.*, vol. 57, pp. 351–61.

Buckner, D. N., and McGrath, J. J. (1963), *Vigilance: a Symposium*, McGraw-Hill.

Bunch, M. E. (1928), 'The effect of electric shock as punishment in human maze learning', *J. comp. Psychol.*, vol. 8, pp. 343–59.

Buss, A. H., and Buss, E. H. (1956), 'The effect of verbal reinforcement combinations on conceptual learning', *J. exp. Psychol.*, vol. 52, pp. 283–7.

Buss, A. H., Braden, W., Orgel, A., and Buss, E. H. (1956), 'Acquisition and extinction with different verbal reinforcement combinations', *J. exp. Psychol.*, vol. 52, pp. 288–95.

Buxton, C. E., and Bakan, M. B. (1949), 'Correction versus non-correction learning techniques as related to reminiscence in serial anticipation learning', *J. exp. Psychol.*, vol. 39, pp. 338–41.

Cameron, E. H., and Steele, W. M. (1905), 'The Poggendorff Illusion', *Psychol. Rev. Monogr. Suppl.*, vol. 7, pp. 83–111.

Campbell, R. A. (1964), 'Feedback and noise-signal detection at three performance levels', *J. acoust. Soc. Am.*, vol. 36, pp. 434–8.

Campbell, R. A., and Small, A. M. (1963), 'Effect of practice and feedback on frequency discrimination', *J. acoust. Soc. Am.*, vol. 35, pp. 1511–14.

Cannon, W. B. (1932), *The Wisdom of the Body,* Norton.

Carr, H. (1930), 'Teaching and learning', *J. genet. Psychol.*, vol. 31, pp. 189–218.

Cason. H. (1932), 'The pleasure-pain theory of learning', *Psychol. Rev.*, vol. 9, pp. 440–66.

Chapanis, A. (1964), 'Knowledge of performance as an incentive in repetitive monotonous tasks', *J. app. Psychol.*, vol. 48, pp. 263–7.

Church, R. M. (1962), 'The effects of competition on reaction time and palmar skin conductance', *J. abnorm. soc. Psychol.*, vol. 65, pp. 32–40.

Church, R. M., and Camp, D. S. (1965), 'Changes in reaction time as a function of knowledge of results', *Am. J. Psychol.*, vol. 78, pp. 102–6.

Church, R. M., Millward, R. B., and Miller, R. (1963), 'Prediction of success in a competitive reaction time situation', *J. abnorm. soc. Psychol.*, vol. 67, pp, 234–40.

Cole, L. W. (1907), 'Concerning the intelligence of racoons', *J. comp. Neur. Psychol.*, vol. 17, p. 235.

Cook, J. O. (1958), 'Supplemeny report: processes underlying learning a simple paired-associate item', *J. exp. Psychol.*, vol. 56, p. 455.

Cook, J. O., and Kendler, T. S. (1956), 'A theoretical model to explain some paired-associate learning data', in Finch G. and Cameron F. (eds.), *Symposium on Air Force Human Engineering Personnel and Training Branch*.

Cook, J. O., and Spitzer, M. E. (1960), 'Supplementary report: prompting vs confirmation in paired associate learning', *J. exp. Psychol.*, vol. 59, pp. 275–6.

Cowles, J. T. (1937), 'Food tokens as incentives for learning by chimpanzees', *Comp. Psychol. Monogr.*, vol. 14, no. 71.

Crafts, L. W., and Gilbert, R. W. (1935), 'The effects of knowledge of results on maze learning and retention', *J. educ. Psychol.*, vol. 26, pp. 177–87.

Crawley, S. L. (1926), 'An experimental investigation of recovery from work', *Arch. Psychol.*, vol. 13, no. 85, p. 66.

Culclasure, D. F. (1964), 'Reinforcement effects in autoinstruction: an intra individual analysis', *Univ. Texas. Dissert. Abstr.*, vol. 25, pp. 287–8.

Dannenberg, R. A. (1965), 'The relationship of intelligence to reinforcement in a linear programmed instruction unit dealing with the free enterprise system', *Univ. Michigan. Diss. Abstr.*, vol. 26, pp. 260–68.

Denny, M. R., Allard, M., Hall, E., and Rokeach, M. (1960), 'Supplementary report: delay of knowledge of results, knowledge of tasks and the intertrial interval', *J. exp. Psychol.*, vol. 60, p. 327.

Driskill, W. E. (1964), 'Partial and continuous feedback in a linear programmed instruction package', in Ofiesh, G. D., and Meierhenry, W. C., *Trends in Programmed Instruction*, D A V I - N E A, N S P I, Washington.

Duncan, K. D. (in press), 'Task analysis evaluated', *Proceedings of N A T O Conference on Current Trends in Programmed Instruction Research*, Nice 1968, Dunod, Paris.

Elwell, J. L., and Grindley, G. C. (1938), 'Effect of knowledge of results on learning and performance', *Brit. J. Psychol.*, vol. 29, pp. 39–54.

English, H. B. (1942), 'How psychology can facilitate military training – a concrete example', *J. appl. Psychol.*, vol. 26, pp. 3–7.

Epstein, W. (1967), *Varieties of Perceptual Learning*, McGraw-Hill.

Eriksen, C. W. (1958), 'Effects of practice with or without correction on discrimination learning', *Am. J. Psychol.*, vol. 71, pp. 350–58.

Evans, J. L. (1960), 'An investigation of teaching machine variables using learning programs in symbolic logic', Doctoral Thesis, University of Pittsburgh.

Evans, G. W. (1964), 'Mode of presentation, pacing, knowledge of results and intellectual level in Automated Instruction', *Oklahoma Univ. Diss. Abstr.*, vol. 25, pp. 1317–18.

Fattu, N. A. (1960), *Training Devices*, Encyclopaedia of Educational Research, Macmillan.

Feldhusen, J. F., and Birt, A., (1962), 'A study of nine methods of presentation of programmed learning material', *J. educ. Res.*, vol. 55, pp. 461–6.

Fitts, P. M. (1962), 'Factors in complex skill training', in Glaser, R. (ed), *Training Research and Education*, University of Pittsburgh Press (reprinted 1965, Science Editions, Wiley).

Frankman, J. P., and Adams, J. A. (1962), 'Theories of vigilance', *Psychol. Bull.*, vol. 59, pp. 257-72.

Freeman, J. T. (1959), 'The effects of reinforced practice on conventional multiple choice tests', *Automated Teaching Bulletin*, vol. 1, pp. 19-20.

Gagné, R. M. (1950), 'Learning and transfer of training from two forms of rudder control test', U S A F H R R C *Res. Note*, 50-1.

Gagné, R. M. (1954), 'Training devices and simulators: some research issues', *Amer. J. Psychol.*, vol. 9, pp. 95-107.

Gibbs, C. B., and Brown I. D. (1955), 'Increased production from the information incentive in a repetitive task', *Manager*, vol. 24, no. 5, pp. 374-9.

Gibson, E. J. (1953), 'A survey of research on improvement in perceptual judgments as a function of controlled practice and training', H R R C *Res. Rep.*, 53-45.

Gilbert, R. W., and Crafts, L. W. (1935), 'The effect of signal for error upon maze learning and retention', *J. exp. Psychol.*, vol. 18, pp. 121-32.

Gleitman, H. (1955), 'Place learning without performance', *J. comp. physiol. Psychol.*, vol. 48, pp. 77-9.

Gordon, N. B. (1968), Personal communication.

Gormezano, L., and Grant, D. A. (1958), 'Progressive ambiguity in the attainment of concepts on the Wisconsin Card Sorting Test', *J. exp. Psychol.*, vol. 55, pp. 621-7.

Green, R. F., Zimilies, H. L., and Spragg, S. D. S. (1955), 'The effects of varying degrees of knowledge of results on knob-setting performance', S P E C D E V C E N *Tech. Rep.*, 241-6-20.

Greenspoon, J. (1955), 'The reinforcing effect of two spoken sounds on the frequency of two responses', *Am. J. Psychol.*, vol. 68, pp. 409-16.

Greenspoon, J. (1965), 'Feedback and the maintenance of verbal responses', *Psychol. Record*, vol. 15, pp. 43–50.

Greenspoon, J., and Foreman, S. (1956), 'Effects of delay of knowledge of results on learning a motor task', *J. exp. Psychol.*, vol. 51, pp. 226–8.

Gundy, R. F. (1961), 'Auditory detection of an unspecified signal', *J. acoust. Soc. Am.*, vol. 33, pp. 1008–12.

Guthrie, E. R. (1935), *The Psychology of Learning*, Harper.

Hamilton, H. C. (1929), 'The effect of incentives on accuracy of discrimination on the Galton Bar', *Arch. Psychol.*, vol. 16, no. 103.

Hauty, G. T., and Payne, R. B. (1955), 'Mitigation of work decrement', *J. exp. Psychol.*, vol. 49, pp. 60–67.

Held, R. (1965), 'Plasticity in sensory-motor systems', *Scientific American*, vol. 213, pp. 89–94.

Heimer, W. L., and Tatz, S. J. (1966), 'Practice effects, knowledge of results and transfer in pitch discrimination', *U.S. Naval Training Device Center*, Tech. Rep. IH–52.

✓ Hilgard, E. R. (1963), 'Issues within learning theory and programmed learning', *Proceedings of 1963 International Conference on Teaching Machines*, Paedagogisches Arbeitstelle, Berlin.

Holding, D. H. (1959), 'Guidance in pursuit tracking', *J. exp. Psychol.*, vol. 47, pp, 362–6.

Holding, D. H. (1965), *Principles of Training*, Pergamon Press.

Holding, D. H., and Macrae, A. W. (1964), 'Guidance, restriction and knowledge of results', *Ergonomics*, vol. 7, pp. 289–95.

Holland, J. G. (1966), 'Research on programming variables', in Glaser, R. (ed.), *Teaching Machines and Programmed Learning II, Data and Directions*, N E A – D A V I, Washington, D.C.

Holtz, W. C., and Azrin, N. H. (1966), 'Conditioning human verbal behaviour', in Honig, W. K. (ed.), *Operant*

Behaviour, Areas of Research and Application, Appleton-Century-Crofts.

Hough, J. B., and Revsin, B. (1963), 'Programmed instruction at the college level: a study of several factors influencing learning', *Phi Delta Kappan*, vol. 44, pp. 286–91.

Houston, R. C. (1947), 'The function of knowledge of results in learning a complex motor skill', Unpubl. M.A. Thesis, Northwestern University, Evanston, Illinois.

Howarth, C. I., and Treisman, M. (1958), 'The effect of warning interval on the electric phosphene and auditory thresholds', *Quart. J. exp. Psychol.*, vol. 10, pp. 130–41.

Hulin, W. S., and Katz, D. (1935), 'A comparison of emphasis upon right and upon wrong responses in learning', *J. exp. Psychol.*, vol. 18, pp. 638–42.

Hull, C. L. (1920), 'Quantitative aspects of the evolution of concepts: an experimental study', *Psychol. Monogr.*, vol. 28, no. 123.

Hull, C. L. (1951), *Essentials of Behavior*, Yale University Press.

Hunt, E. B., Marin, J., and Stone, P. J. (1966), *Experiments in Induction*, Academic Press.

Jacobs, P. I., and Kulkarni, S. (1966), 'A test of some assumptions underlying programmed instruction', *Psychol. Rep.*, vol. 18, pp. 103–10.

James, W. H., and Rotter, J. B. (1958), 'Partial and 100 per cent reinforcement under chance and skill conditions', *J. exp. Psychol.*, vol. 55, pp. 397–403.

Johanson, A. M. (1922), 'The influence of incentives and punishment on reaction time', *Arch. Psychol.*, vol. 8, p. 54.

Johnson, D. M. (1944), 'Generalization of a scale of values by the averaging of practice effects', *J. exp. Psychol.*, vol. 34, pp. 425–36.

Johnson, D. M. (1946), 'How a person establishes a scale for evaluating his performance', *J. exp. Psychol.*, vol. 36, pp. 25–34.

Johnson, D. M. (1949), 'Learning function for a change in the scale of judgment', *J. exp. Psychol.*, vol. 39, pp. 851–60.

Judd, C. H. (1902), 'Practice and its effects on the perception of illusions', *Psychol. Rev.*, vol. 9, pp. 27–39.

Judd, C. H. (1904), 'The Müller-Lyer Illusion', *Psychol. Rev. Monogr. Suppl.*, vols. 6–7, pp. 55–81.

Kanfer, F. H. (1968), 'Verbal conditioning: A review of its current status', in Dixon, J. R., and Horton, D. L., *Verbal Behaviour and General Behaviour Theory*, Prentice-Hall, pp. 254–90.

Karlin, L. (1960), 'Psychological study of motor skills: Phase I', U.S. Navy Tech. Rep. NAVTRADEVCEN 558–1.

Karlin, L., and Mortimer, R. G. (1961), 'Psychological study of motor skills: Phase II', U.S. Navy Tech. Rep. NAVTRADEVCEN 558–2.

Kelley, C. R. (1960), 'Developing and testing the effectiveness of the "Predictor Instrument"', Office of Naval Research, Tech. Rep. 252–60–1.

Koch, H. L. (1924), 'The influence of mechanical guidance on maze learning', *Psychol. Monogr.*, No. 33.

Koch, H. L. (1930), 'Some factors affecting the relative efficiency of certain modes of presenting material for memorising', *Am. J. Psychol.*, vol. 42, pp. 370–88.

Kosofski, S. (1952), 'The effectiveness of positive and negative guidance as related to the degree of organisation of the material to be learned', *J. genet. Psychol.*, vol. 47, pp. 91–104.

Krasner, L. (1958), 'Studies of the conditioning of verbal behaviour', *Psychol. Bull.*, vol. 55, pp. 147–70.

Krumboltz, J. D., and Kiesler, C. A. (1965), 'The partial reinforcement paradigm and programmed instruction', *J. prog. Instr.*, vol. 3, pp. 9–14.

Lee, B. S. (1950), 'Effects of delayed speech feedback', *J. acoust. soc. Am.*, vol. 22, pp. 824–6.

Lee, B. S. (1951), 'Artificial Stutter', *J. speech. hear. Dis.*, vol. 16, pp. 53–5.

Levine, M., Leitenberg, H., and Richter, M. (1964), 'The blank trials law: the equivalence of positive reinforcement and non-reinforcement', *Psychol. Rev.*, vol. 71, pp. 94–103.

Lewis, B. N., Horabin, I.S., and Gane, L. P. (1967), *Flow Charts, Logical Trees and Algorithms for Rules and Regulations*, H.M.S.O.

Lincoln, R. S. (1954),'Learning a rate of movement', *J. exp. Psychol.*, vol. 47, pp. 465–70.

Lincoln, R. S. (1956), 'Learning and retaining a rate of movement with the aid of kinaesthetic and verbal cues', *J. exp. Psychol.*, vol. 51, pp. 199–204.

Lindahl, L. G. (1945), 'Movement analysis as an industrial training method', *J. appl. Psychol.*, vol. 29, pp. 420–30.

Locke, E. A. (1966a), 'The relationship of intentions to level of performance', *J. appl. Psychol.*, vol. 50, pp. 60–66.

Locke, E. A. (1966b), 'A closer look at level of aspiration as a training procedure: a re-analysis of Fryer's data', *J. appl. Psychol.*, vol. 50, pp. 417–20.

Locke, E. A., and Bryan, J. F. (1966a), 'Cognitive aspects of psychomotor performance: the effects of performance goals on level of performance', *J. appl. Psychol.*, vol. 50, pp. 286–91.

Locke, E. A., and Bryan, J. F. (1966b), 'The effects of goal-setting, rule learning and knowledge of score on performance', *Am. J. Psychol.*, vol. 79, pp. 451–7.

Loeb, M., and Dickson, J. (1961), 'Factors influencing the practice effect of auditory thresholds', *J. acoust. Soc. Am.*, vol. 33, pp. 917–21.

Lorge, I., and Thorndike, E. L. (1935), 'The influence of delay in the after-effect of a connection', *J. exp. Psychol.*, vol. 18, pp. 186–94.

Ludgate, K. E. (1923), 'The effect of manual guidance upon maze learning', *Psychol. Monogr.*, vol. 35, no. 1.

Lukaszewski, J. S., and Elliott, D. N. (1961), 'Auditory threshold as a function of forced-choice techniques, feedback and motivation', *J. acoust. Soc. Am.*, vol. 33, pp. 1046–54.

McDonald, F. J., and Allen, D., (1962), 'An investigaion of presentation, response and correction factors in programmed instruction', *J. educ. Res.*, vol. 55, pp. 502–7.

McGuigan, E. J. (1959), 'The effect of precision, delay, and schedule of knowledge of results on performance', *J. exp. Psychol.*, vol. 58, pp. 79–84.

Mace, C. A. (1935), 'Incentives: some experimental studies', *Indust. Health Res. Bd. Rept.*, no. 72.

Mackworth, N. H. (1950), 'Researches on the measurement of human performance', *Med. Res. Council Special Report*, no. 268.

Marx, M. H., and Goodson, F. E. (1956), 'Further gradients of error reinforcement following repeated reinforced responses', *J. exp. Psychol.*, vol. 51, pp. 421–8.

Meyer, S. R. (1960), 'Report on the initial test of a junior high school vocabulary program', in Lumsdaine, A. A., and Glaser, R. (eds.), *Teaching Machines and Programmed Learning*, NEA–DAVI, Washington, pp. 229–46.

Michael, D. N., and Maccoby, N. (1961), 'Factors influencing the effects of student participation on verbal learning from film: Motivating vs practice effects, "feedback" and overt vs covert responding', in Lumsdaine, A. A. (ed.), *Student response in Programmed Instruction*, NAS–NRC, Washington.

Miller, R. B. (1953), 'Handbook of training and equipment design', *WADC Technical Report*, 53–136.

Miller, G. A., Galanter, E., and Pribram, K. H. (1960), *Plans and the Structure of Behavior*, Holt.

Moers, M. (1924), 'Ein Beitrag zur Untersuchung der Augenmasprüfung', *Arch. z. angew. Psychol.*, vol. 23, pp. 257–92.

Moore, J. W., and Halpern, J. (1967), 'Three-stimulus two-choice auditory discrimination learning with blank trials', *J. exp. Psychol.*, vol. 73, pp. 241–6.

Moore, J. W., and Smith, W. J. (1961), 'Knowledge of

results in self-teaching spelling', *Psychol. Rep.*, vol. 9, pp. 717–26.

Moore, J. W., and Smith, W. J. (1964), 'Role of knowledge of results in programmed instruction', *Psychol. Rep.*, vol. 14, pp. 407–23.

Morgan, C. T., Cook, J. S., Chapanis, A., and Lund, M. W. (1963), *Human Engineering Guide to Equipment Design*, McGraw-Hill.

Morin, R. E. (1951), 'The function of informative feedback and rewarding feedback in acquisition of a lever positioning habit', H R R C *Res. Note P and M S*, 51–11.

Morin, R. E., and Gagné, R. M. (1951), 'Pedestal sight manipulation test performance as influenced by variations in type and amount of psychological feedback', *U S A F* H R R C *Res. Note P and M S*, 51–7.

Nuttin, J. (1953), *Tâche, Réussite, et Échec*, Publications Universitaires, Louvain.

Oppenheim, N. (1964), 'The relation between intelligence and difference patterns of feedback in a linear teaching program', *Columbia Univ. Dissert. Abstr.*, vol. 25, p. 2857.

Opsahl, R. L., and Dunnette, M. D. (1966), 'The role of financial compensation in industrial motivation', *Psychol. Bull.*, vol. 66, pp. 94–118.

Ottina, J. R. (1964), 'The effects of delay in knowledge of results on the amount learned in teaching machine programs of differing cue content', *Univ. Southern Calif. Dissert. Abstr.*, vol. 25, p. 1753.

Parkinson, B. P. (1964), 'The effect of an extended post information feedback interval, anxiety and ability on programmed learning with college students', *Univ. Utah. Dissert. Abstr.*, vol. 25, pp. 1753–4.

Pask, G. (1961), *An Approach to Cybernetics*, Hutchinson.

Pavlov, I. P. (1927), *Conditioned Reflexes* (trans. by G. V. Anrep), Oxford University Press.

Payne, R. B., and Hauty, G. T. (1955), 'Effects of psychological feedback upon work decrement', *J. exp. Psychol.*, vol. 50, pp. 342–51.

Phares, E. J. (1957), 'Expectancy changes in skill and chance situations', *J. abnorm. soc. Psychol.*, vol. 54, pp. 339–42.

Postman, L. (1947), 'The history and present status of the Law of Effect', *Psychol. Bull.*, vol. 44, pp. 489–563.

Postman, L. (1964), *Psychology in the Making*, Alfred A. Knopf.

Poulton, E. C. (1966), 'Tracking behaviour', in Bilodeau, E. A. (ed.), *Acquisition of Skill*, Academic Press, pp. 361–410.

Pressey, S. L. (1926), 'A simple apparatus which gives test and scores – and teaches', *School and Society*, vol. 23, pp. 373–6.

Pressey, S. L. (1927), 'A machine for automatic teaching of drill material', *School and Society*, vol. 25, pp. 549–52.

Pressey, S. L. (1950), 'Development and appraisal of devices providing immediate automatic scoring of objective tests and concomitant self-instruction', *J. Psychol.*, vol. 29, pp. 417–47.

Pubols, B. H. (1960), 'Incentive magnitude, learning and performance in animals', *Psychol. Bull.*, vol. 57, pp. 89–115.

Rexroad, C. N. (1926), 'Administering electric shock for inaccuracy in continuous multiple-choice reactions', *J. exp. Psychol.*, vol. 9, pp. 1–18.

Ripple, R. E., (1963), 'Comparison of the effectiveness of a programmed text with three other methods of presentation', *Psychol. Rep.*, vol. 12, pp. 227–37.

Ross, C. C. (1927), 'An experiment in motivation', *J. educ. Psychol.*, vol. 18, pp. 337–46.

Russell, W. A. (1952), 'Retention of verbal material as a function of motivating instructions and experimentally induced failure', *J. exp. Psychol.*, vol. 43, pp. 207–16.

Sackett, R. S. (1947), 'The effect of knowledge of scores on learning a simulated tracking problem', *Amer. J. Psychol.*, vol. 2, p. 299.

Saltzman, I. J. (1951), 'Delay of reward and human

verbal learning', *J. exp. Psychol.*, vol. 41, pp. 437–9.

Seashore, R. H. (1951), 'Work and motor performance', in Stevens, S. S. (ed.), *Handbook of Experimental Psychology*, Wiley, pp. 1341–62.

Seashore, R. H., and Bavelas, A. (1941), 'The functioning of knowledge of results in Thorndike's line-drawing experiment', *Psychol. Rev.*, vol. 48, pp. 155–64.

Seashore, R. H. Underwood, B. J., Berks, J., and Houston, R. C. (1949), 'The effect of knowledge of results on performance in the SAM pedestal sight manipulation test', in Underwood, B. J., *Experimental Psychology*, Appleton-Century-Crofts, pp. 414–17.

Seymour, W. D. (1954), *Industrial Training for Manual Operations*, Pitman.

Seymour, W. D. (1966), *Industrial Skills*, Pitman.

Shafer, L., and Murphy, G. (1943), 'The role of autism in a figure-ground relationship', *J. exp. Psychol.*, vol. 32, pp. 335–43.

Shannon, C. E., and Weaver, W. (1949), *The Mathematical Theory of Communication*, University of Illinois Press.

Sheffield, F. D. (1949), 'Spread of effect without reward or learning', *J. exp. Psychol.*, vol. 39, pp. 575–9.

Sidley, N. A., Winograd, E., and Bedauf, E. W. (1965), 'Stimulus identification overlap in learning to identify complex sounds', *J. acoust. Soc. Am.*, vol. 38, pp. 11–13.

Skinner, B. F. (1953), *Science and Human Behavior*, Macmillan.

Skinner, B. F. (1954), 'The science of learning and the art of teaching', *Harvard Educ. Rev.*, vol. 24, pp. 86–97.

Skinner, B. F. (1958), 'Teaching machines', *Science*, vol. 128, pp. 969–77.

Smith, K. U. (1962), *Delayed Sensory Feedback and Behavior*, Saunders, Philadelphia.

Smith, K. U., and Smith, W. M. (1962), *Perception and Motion: An Analysis of Space-Structured Behavior*, Saunders, Philadelphia.

Smode, A. E. (1958), 'Learning and performance in a tracking task under two levels of achievement information feedback', *J. exp. Psychol.*, vol. 56, pp. 297–304.

Spencer, H. (1872), *Principles of Psychology*, Williams and Norgate, London.

Stockbridge, H. W. C., and Chambers, B. (1958), 'Aiming, transfer of training and knowledge of results', *J. appl. Psychol.*, vol. 42, pp. 148–53.

Stratton, G. M. (1896), 'Some preliminary experiments in vision without inversion of the retinal image', *Psychol. Rev.*, vol. 3, pp. 611–17.

Stratton, G. M. (1897), 'Vision without inversion of the retinal image', *Psychol. Rev.*, vol. 4, pp. 341–60 and 463–81.

Swets, J. (1962), 'Learning to identify nonverbal sounds: an application of a computer as a teaching machine', *U.S. Naval Training Device Center*, Tech. Rep. no. 789–1.

Swets, J. A., Harris, J. S., McElroy, L. S., and Rudloe, H. (1964), 'Further experiments on computer-aided learning of sound identification', *U.S. Naval Training Device Center*, Tech. Rep. no. 789–2.

Swets, J. A., and Sewell, S. T. (1963), 'Invariance of signal detectability over stages of practice and levels of motivation', *J. exp. Psychol.*, vol. 66, pp. 120–26.

Taylor, F. V., and Birmingham, H. P. (1948), 'Studies in tracking behavior. II. The acceleration pattern of quick manual corrective responses', *J. exp. Psychol.*, vol. 38, pp. 783–95.

Thorndike, E. L. (1898), 'Animal intelligence', *Psychol. Rev. Monogr. Suppl. 2, No. 8.*

Thorndike, E. L. (1911), *Animal Intelligence: Experimental Studies*, Macmillan.

Thorndike, E. L. (1931), *Human Learning*, Century (reprinted 1966, M.I.T. Press).

Thorndike, E. L. (1932), *The Fundamentals of Learning*, Teacher's College, Columbia University.

Thorndike, E. L. (1933a), '*An Experimental Study of*

Rewards', Teacher's College, Columbia University, publication no. 580.

Thorndike, E. L. (1933b), 'A theory of the action of the after-effects of a connection upon it', *Psychol. Rev.*, vol. 40, p. 434–89.

Thorndike, E. L., and Lorge, I. (1935), 'The influence of relevance and belonging', *J. exp. Psychol.*, vol 18, pp. 574–84.

Thorndike, E. L., and Woodworth, R. S. (1901), 'Influence of improvement in one verbal function upon the efficiency of other functions', *Psychol. Rev.*, vol. 8, pp. 247–61, 384–95, 553–64.

Tilton, J. W. (1939), 'The effect of "right" and "wrong" upon the learning of nonsense syllables in a multiple-choice arrangement', *J. educ. Psychol.*, vol. 30, pp. 95–115.

Tilton, J. W. (1945), 'Gradients of effect', *J. genet. Psychol.*, vol 66, pp. 3–19.

Tolman, E. C. (1938), 'The Law of Effect', *Psychol. Rev.*, vol. 45, pp. 200–203.

Tolman, E. C., Hall, C. S., and Bretnall, E. P. (1932), 'A disproof of the Law of Effect and a substitution of the law of emphasis, motivation and disruption', *J. exp. Psychol.*, vol. 15, pp. 601–14.

Tombaugh, T. N., and Marx, M. H. (1963), 'The effects of increasing and decreasing orders of monetary incentive on resistance to extinction in children', *Psychol. Rec*; vol. 13, pp. 187–90.

Toppen, J. T. (1965a), 'Effect of size and frequency of money reinforcement on human operant (work) behaviour', *Percept. mot. Skills*, vol. 20, pp. 259–69.

Toppen, J. T. (1965b), 'Money reinforcement and human operant (work) behaviour: II. Within-subject comparisons', *Percept. mot. Skills*, vol. 20, pp. 1193–9.

Toppen, J. T. (1965c), 'Money reinforcement and human operant (work) behaviour: III. Piece work-payment and time-payment comparisons', *Percept. mot. Skills*, vol. 21, pp. 907–13.

Toppen, J. T. (1966), 'Money reinforcement and human operant (work) behaviour: IV. Temporarily extended within-subject's comparisons', *Percept. mot. Skills*, vol. 22, pp. 575–81.

Travis, R. C. (1938), 'Comparison of the influence of monetary reward and electric shocks on learning in eye-hand coordination', *J. exp. Psychol.*, vol. 23, pp. 423–7.

Trowbridge, M. H., and Cason, H. (1932), 'An experimental study of Thorndike's Theory of Learning', *J. gen. Psychol.*, vol. 7, pp. 245–58.

von Wright, J. M. (1957), 'A note on the role of guidance in learning', *Brit. J. Psychol.*, vol. 48, pp. 133–7.

Wallach, H., and Henle, M. (1941), 'An experimental analysis of the Law of Effect', *J. exp. Psychol.*, vol. 28, pp. 340–49.

Wallach, H., and Henle, M. (1942), 'A further study of the function of reward', *J. exp. Psychol.*, vol. 30, pp. 147–60.

Wang, G. H. (1925), 'The influence of tuition on the acquisition of skill', *Psychol. Monogr.*, vol. 34, no. 154.

Waters, R. H. (1930), 'The influence of large amounts of manual guidance upon human learning', *J. gen. Psychol.*, vol. 4, pp. 213–27.

Waters, R. H. (1933), 'The specificity of knowledge of results and improvement', *Psychol. Bull.*, vol. 30, p. 673.

Wiener, N. (1948), *Cybernetics or Control and Communication in the Animal and the Machine*, Wiley.

Williams, M. C. (1902), 'Normal illusion in representative geometrical forms', *Univ. Iowa. Stud. Psychol.*, vol. 3, pp. 38–139.

Wolfe, D. (1951), 'Training', in Stevens, S. S. (ed.), *Handbook of Experimental Psychology*, Wiley, pp. 1267–86.

Wolfe, H. K. (1923), 'On the estimation on the middle of lines', *Amer. J. Psychol.*, vol. 34, pp. 313–58.

Woodworth, R. S. (1899), 'The accuracy of voluntary movement', *Psychol. Monogr.*, vol. 3, no. 3.

Wyatt, S. (1934), *Incentives in repetitive work: A practical experiment in a factory* (Industrial Health Research Board Report no. 69), H.M.S.O., London.

Zwislocki, J., Maire, F., Feldman, A. S., and Rubin, H. (1958), 'On the effect of practice and motivation on the thershold of audibility' *J. acoust. Soc. Am.*, vol. 30, pp. 254–62.

Index

Penguin science of behaviour

Published simultaneously

On the experience of time

Robert E. Ornstein

Time is a continuing, compelling and universal experience. We continually feel time passing but where does it come from? We continually experience it, but we cannot taste it, see it, smell it, hear it, or touch it. How then *do* we experience time? What do we *use* to experience it?

In a series of remarkable experiments, Dr Ornstein shows that it is difficult to maintain an 'inner clock' explanation of the experience of time and postulates a cognitive, information processing approach. This approach alone makes sense out of the very difficult data of the experience of time, and in particular of the experience of duration – the lengthening of duration under LSD, for example, or the effects of a 'successful' or a 'failure' experience, time in sensory deprivation, the time-order effect, or the influence of the administration of a sedative or stimulant drug.

As Professor Pribram writes in his Editorial Foreword 'Ornstein's approach to the analysis of the time experience makes eminent sense. Besides this, Ornstein's experiments are ingenious and his approach is fun to read about and to contemplate. Fun should be shared – so here is Ornstein on the experience of time.'

Dr Robert Evan Ornstein is the Research Psychologist at the Langley-Porter Neuropsychiatric Institute, San Francisco, California.

Penguin science of behaviour

Forthcoming titles

Selective listening
Neville Moray
(To be published September 1969)

Vigilance and habituation
Jane Mackworth
(To be published September 1969)

Vigilance and attention
Jane Mackworth
(To be published February 1970)

Penguin modern psychology readings

Experiments in visual perception

Edited by M. D. Vernon

Experiments in Visual Perception concentrates on the major
problems of experiments in the psychology of vision.
Professor Vernon revues four central topics – the perception
of form, space and distance, 'constancy' phenomena, and
movement – and then explains the variations in perception
which occur within the individual and between individuals.
Four excerpts from Piaget on perception in infancy complete
the volume.

Motivation

Edited by Dalbir Bindra and Jane Stewart

Since the 1930s motivation has been an area of active research
in psychology. The papers collected in this volume are among
those that deal most directly with the three central problems
of motivation: *drive* – what instigates an organism to action?
goal direction – what directs behaviour towards certain ends?
reinforcement – what precisely makes events rewarding and
others punishing? In *Motivation* the papers and editorial
comments provide a coherent account of the development of
theoretical ideas that guide current experimental work on
these problems.

Verbal learning and memory

Edited by Leo Postman and Geoffrey Keppel

This collection of readings reflects both the historical
continuity in research and the innovation and change that has
taken place in psychological study of verbal learning and
memory in the last twenty years. Although traditional
distinctions are maintained – acquisition of verbal materal, its
recall, the phenomena of interference and transfer – the
common developments in experimental analysis of these
problems are demonstrated.

Penguin modern psychology readings

Recent titles

Brain and behaviour (4 volumes)
Edited by K. H. Pribram
1 Mood, states and mind
2 Perception and action
3 Memory mechanisms
4 Adaptation

Cross-cultural studies
Edited by D. R. Price-Williams

Psychology and the visual arts
Edited by James Hogg

Forthcoming titles

Experimental psychology in industry
Edited by D. H. Holding
(To be published October 1969)

Skills
Edited by David Legge
(To be published February 1970)